Solidarity Forever

An oral history of the IWW

Mourn not the dead

by Ralph Chaplin

Mourn not the dead that in the cool earth lie—
    Dust unto dust—
The calm sweet earth that mothers all who die
    As all men must;

Mourn not your captive comrades who must dwell—
    Too strong to strive—
Within each steel bound coffin of a cell,
    Buried alive;

But rather mourn the apathetic throng—
    The cowed and the meek—
Who see the world's great anguish and its wrong
    And dare not speak!

Solidarity Forever

An oral history of the IWW

Stewart Bird
Dan Georgakas
Deborah Shaffer

LAKE VIEW Press

Chicago

ISBN 0-941702-11-1 (hard)
ISBN 0-941702-12-X (soft)
Library of Congress
Catalog Card Number:
84-8291

Lake View Press
Chicago

The Wobblies, the film for which most of the interviews contained within were made, is available from
First Run Features
153 Waverly Place
NY, NY 10014
212-243-0600

Appearing in the film are:
Jack Miller, Joe Murphy, Sophie Cohen, Irma Lombardi, Violet Miller, Dominic Mignone, Tom Scribner, James Fair, Angelo Rocco, Nels Peterson, Irv Hanson, Katie Pintek, Nicolaas Steelink, Art Shields, Fred Thompson, Sam Krieger, Vaino Konga, Mike Foudy, and Utah Phillips.

Table of Contents

THE I.W.W. is COMING!

JOIN THE ONE BIG UNION

You don't remember the
Wobblies. You were too young.
Or else not even born yet.
There has never been anything
like them, before or since.
—James Jones
From Here to Eternity

THE IWW
RECONSIDERED

Millions of Americans enjoy liberties off and on the job that were championed by an organization most of them are unfamiliar with—the Industrial Workers of the World. But when the twentieth century was still a newborn, the IWW was a mass popular movement whose challenges to established economic and social power made headlines from coast to coast. Employers considered its demands preposterous, bigots recoiled from its fervent democratic spirit, and established trade unions feared its radicalism. These foes of the IWW united and struck back at the organization in an effort that was capped by an unprecedented campaign of legal terrorism directed by the federal government. Although this assault destabilized the IWW and sent many of its members to prison, the momentum for social change energized by the IWWs (more commonly known as Wobblies) was not permanently derailed.[1] IWW veterans became activists in newer and larger mass organizations. IWW songs and IWW tactics were taken wholecloth or in revised forms for new social struggles. The itinerant Wobbly hopping on a moving freight car became identified as the quintessential native American rebel.

Since the 1960s, some excellent histories and collections of IWW writing have made it possible to think about how the IWW experience might relate to ongoing and future social movements.[2] In the mid-1970s, Stewart Bird and Deborah Shaffer contributed to this historical inquiry by filming interviews with IWWs who had been active during the organization's glory years. The filmmakers wanted to let these men and women, many of them in their eighties and nineties, tell in their own words what it had meant to be a Wobbly. By combining these oral histories with period photographs, IWW music, historical newsreels, and other materials, Bird and Shaffer hoped their film, *The Wobblies*, would reanimate for new generations a sense of the passion that had once mobilized working America.[3]

As their research progressed, Bird and Shaffer became convinced that the IWW was the finest expression of an indigenous radical tradition. They also concluded that the federal program to destroy the IWW was the historic prototype later employed against other movements for social change. In this light, the testimonies of rank and file Wobblies, ordinary workers who had been the blood and sinew of the IWW, seemed all the more important to preserve and understand. The present book carries forward those concerns by providing longer oral histories from IWWs featured in the film, interviews not included in the film, additional photographic documentation of the IWW, and the kind of statistical and historic detailing that is awkward in cinema. Our view is that Americans interested in social justice can profit greatly by examining the IWW for a way of being that might once again inspire the American imagination.

When some two hundred men and women convened on June 27, 1905, to found the IWW, the United States was still an adolescent nation freshly emerged from its status as a frontier society and not yet recognized as a major world power. Geronimo had led his last Apache war party less than twenty years earlier; digging on the Panama Canal had just commenced; and Oklahoma, New Mexico, and Arizona were not yet states. The American Federation of Labor, already twenty-five years old, considered itself a remarkable success for having managed to organize a million and a half workers. Although recent European immigration had helped to swell the national population to eighty-two million, the AFL was not at all embarassed that many of its locals excluded non-whites, women, the unskilled, and the foreign-born. The IWW founders who gathered in Chicago, railroad hub of industrial and agricultural America, had a national and world vision which markedly set them apart from their AFL brethren. William D. Haywood, then Secretary of the Western Federation of Miners, brought the convention to order with words that promised a second American Revolution: "Fellow workers, this is the Continental Congress of the working class."[4]

Of prime concern to the delegates were needs rooted in the realities of everyday American life. The surplus of labor had grown so great that in most years millions of laborers were forced to drift from job to job, virtually defenseless before the dictates of employers, certain only of regular unemployment. Most Americans sought full-time work at age fourteen, and a good many others were forced to seek employment when half that age. Individuals who did find stable jobs often had to suffer wages that were at subsistence level and conditions that were ruinous to their health.

Employers were intractable in their resistance to working class organization. They did not recognize the right of their workers to bargain collectively if a majority so desired, much less their right to strike or picket. When workers did attempt to organize themselves, employers did not hesitate to use violent countermeasures. Few strikes took place without loss of life. The resulting bitterness had made the prospect of fundamental change appealing to most workers, and nearly every prominent labor radical came to the founding convention of the IWW in hopes of uniting behind a specific agenda. One of the opening addresses was made by Eugene V. Debs, famed for his leadership of a national railroad strike broken by federal troops and soon to win nearly a million votes as the presidential candidate of the rapidly growing Socialist Party.[5]

The program adopted by the convention and later elaborated proved to be a unique blend of trade union and radical ideology. The IWW preamble, which served as a declaration of principles, stated that the working class and the employing class had nothing in common. The solution to economic and social injustice in America and in the world lay in the creation of a worker-controlled political system termed "industrial democracy." The priority task was to create industrial unions under the banner of the "One Big Union," the IWW. These industrial unions would fight for gains in the existing system until the IWW was strong enough to call a general strike that would bring all economic activity to a standstill. The condition for returning to work would be the substitution of industrial unions for all business enterprises and governmental agencies. The means of production would then be run by the unions to satisfy social needs rather than private profit. What had been done in one country would eventually take place in all nations. This vision of a peaceful and democratic revolution would soon touch the lives of millions of Americans, inspiring both incredible devotion and awesome hostility.

The IWW was to pass through four phases of decidedly different complexion. From its founding through about 1911, the organization refined its distinctive orientation and strove to establish viable local units. During this period, the IWW achieved renown for its tenaciously fought strikes and fights for freedom of speech. At the same time, it lost the support of industrial unionists solely interested in reform. Beginning with a sensational, but short-lived triumph in textiles in 1912, the IWW began to be increasingly effective as a trade union, winning tremendous support among harvest workers, lumberjacks, miners, longshoremen, and mariners. This spectacular growth was choked off in 1917 by the largest federal and state effort to destroy an American political organization yet seen. The rationale offered was that Wobbly agitation during wartime was equivalent to treason. Relentless governmental hounding of the IWW forced the organization into a defensive posture with most of its energies going to legal defense of its leadership and its very right to exist. Ideological disputes set off by the suppression, the birth of an American Communist movement, and infiltration by government and company agents led to an organizational schism in 1924. From that year onward, the IWW became an increasingly marginal political force with pronounced anarchist overtones, while simultaneously becoming ever more popular as a subject for mythmaking.[6]

THE COMMONWEALTH OF TOIL

Industrial unions were the major building blocks of the IWW. Wobblies insisted that the craft unionism of the AFL, derided as the "American Separation of Labor," was outdated. Craft unions fragmented labor's power into small competing units that had to struggle with employers who had organized their power into national industrial associations and corporations. Some unions within the AFL, such as the Brewers, and some independent unions, such as the gutsy Western Federation of Miners, already practised industrial unionism. The IWW argued that all the old craft unions and all new unions should adopt this form of organization.

Viewed from the present, when industrial unions are a dominant form of organized labor, the IWW proposal seems modest. But in the early 1900s, industrial unions were an alarming prospect to many employers, politicians and established trade unionists. Not the least upsetting was the IWW's dedication to organizing all workers in absolute solidarity; these included all those sections of labor the AFL had more or less abandoned. The IWW planned to carry out its program at a time when American capitalism was at its most unbridled stage of development and when the working class, native and foreign-born, was still adjusting to urbanized society.

The industrial unions envisioned by the IWW were fundamentally different from the reformist industrial unions of that time or of the kind that came into existence with the Congress of Industrial Organization (CIO) in the 1930s. Reformers saw industrial unions as more effective mechanisms for getting labor a bigger share of the capitalist pie. The IWW proposed to have the unions bake a whole new pie for workers only. For Wobblies, building unions was a way of building a new society in the shell of the old. Strikes and other militant actions were just so many battles in a class war, with any settlement a temporary ceasefire. The ultimate goal was not a favorable contract, but a reordering of society.

Tension between revolutionaries and reformers manifested itself in countless disagreements over tactics. The most bitter of these within the ranks of the IWW itself involved those who urged the IWW to have a political arm and those who argued that the basic power of workers was at the point of production. The direct actionists believed that job control was the speediest route to the new society. The idea of capturing power at the ballot box, as urged by Socialist allies, was not particularly attractive to them at a time when the majority of workers were barred from the polls. All women, all the many workers under twenty-one, and all unnaturalized foreign-born workers—the vast majority of working America—were legally disenfranchised. In those parts of the United States where black labor was dominant, procedural harassments and outright intimidation kept most blacks from voting. Other large blocks of workers—seamen, itinerants, and lumberjacks—were unable to maintain registration at fixed polling sites. To place labor's hope on the ballot box seemed to select a field of combat where working class power was at its minimum, instead of concentrating on the point of production where its power was maximal.

The third IWW convention in 1908 resolved the dispute in favor of direct action. Leading the victorious faction was Vincent St. John, a founder of the Western Federation of Miners and the man who would lead the IWW for the next seven years. But adopting direct action as the IWW's major form of struggle did not end all political sentiment within the organization. Many Wobblies maintained cordial relationships with militant Socialists and, particularly in the mining camps, IWW-oriented workers took part in local and state electoral campaigns. In a real sense, the sentiment for some political presence was eclipsed rather than extinguished. As late as 1924, LaFollette for President buttons could be seen at IWW national headquarters.[7]

Exactly what direct action encompassed depended upon which Wobbly one spoke with, when, and where, but direct action always entailed an immediate assertion of worker power in the work place. Slowdowns and strikes of every kind were the most common form. Whether violent acts were acceptable remained unclear, and IWW speakers further complicated the issue of violence by frequently urging the workers to commit "sabotage" without ever precisely defining that term. Most IWW literature stressed that workers had to use mental dynamite by demonstrating with their fists in their pockets, but some IWW songs and some IWW literature implied that circumstances might arise where violence could not be ruled out.[8] The reality was that the IWW consciously used "direct action" and "sabotage" somewhat ambiguously, in much the way civil rights activists of the 1960s found it useful to employ the vague but menacing phrase "by any means necessary."

In the forge of strikes involving thousands of workers, the IWW proved to be remarkably non-violent in a most violent age. Wobblies understood that employers used violent incidents to turn public opinion against strikers and as an excuse to call in the military. Whenever violence did take place during IWW-led strikes, subsequent investigations invariably traced it back to provocateurs hired by the employers. Aversion to violence was further reenforced by the knowledge that any incident could result in the jailing of union leaders. The justification advanced for such jailings was that the union had instigated a mob action, and thus its leaders, even if not outright conspirators, were ultimately responsible for any illegal acts resulting from their agitation. Such reasoning did not hold up in most courts, but the jailing of leaders could behead a strike at a most critical moment and tip the immediate balance of power in favor of the employers.

An ironic aspect of the violence controversy was that while IWWs spoke openly about sabotage, other supposedly conservative unions were more apt to practice it. AFL craftspeople broke machinery they thought would make their skills obsolete, and construction unions within the AFL had secret dynamite squads to be used as a last resort. Locals of the Western Federation of Miners had military drill teams and stockpiled ammunition.[9]

Working out the full implications of direct action led to unusual IWW positions on conventional union practices. Wobblies strove to concentrate as much power as possible in individual members and locals. This led them to oppose the system by which union dues are automatically subtracted from a paycheck and sent to the union by the company. IWWs felt this insulated leaders from immediate accountability and fostered an unhealthy dependence on management's bureaucracy. Wobblies also wanted to keep dues and fees as low as possible, so that no worker would be discouraged from membership on economic grounds. Regular deductions for health and life insurance were barred as well. The IWWs believed the coming social revolution would provide ultimate solutions to such needs. In the interim, there could be special collections to meet emergencies.

The IWW policy against written contracts also stemmed from the philosophy of direct action. Contracts with different craft unions in the same industry usually expired at different times of the year, making united strike action impossible. Wobblies reasoned that the length of any contract, even with an industrial union, was artificially set and likely to elapse at a time when it was difficult for workers to react militantly. Experience had shown that management devised various means to get around contractual restraints whenever it felt strong enough to do so. As a result, the IWW opted for non-contractual agreements without any time boundaries. This left workers free to act directly for more gains whenever they felt able. Benefits already won would be safeguarded by the same worker solidarity that had won them in the first place. Refusal to sign contracts, to accept dues checkoffs, and to build huge treasuries made the vitality of the union absolutely dependent upon the commitment of the rank and file. It also meant that the daily operation of any local was cumbersome and that funds for minimal services could become dangerously low when there was no crisis.

By far the most spectacular form of direct action in the early years was the IWW's massive civil disobedience to unjust laws. This activity was triggered by the need to reach migratory workers at transportation hubs, hiring centers and towns where they rested between jobs. Before the age of radio, public speaking of all kinds was a major means of mass communication, and soapbox orators often displayed their rhetorical skills on street corners and in public squares. When Wobblies proved to be persuasive "jawsmiths" in such settings, employers began to press city officials to drive them from all public places, a clear violation of several provisions of the First Amendment to the Constitution. The IWW responded by calling for all sympathizers to travel to the affected city and exercise their constitutional rights at a particular site. Instead of avoiding the authorities, free speechers were to go to jail, the object being to flood the facilities with so many bodies that the city would be financially and politically unable to enforce its illegal mandates.

Free speech fights were pure direct action. An individual who wanted the right to speak in public did not wait for a local ordinance to be tested in faraway courts in a process that might take years; he or she simply got up and personally exercised the disputed right, thereby making an immediate and direct appeal to fellow citizens. By extending or withholding solidarity, a community quickly determined the boundaries of civil liberties. The first free speech fight led by the IWW took place in the summer of 1909 in Missoula, Montana. Over two dozen more followed in the next six years, most ending in clearcut victories.[10] This bold assertion of basic American freedoms was supported by many groups and individuals, including some of a conservative orientation who were otherwise not sympathetic to the IWW credo.

At The Point of Production

For nearly a decade the IWW made little headway in organizing basic industry. Landmark strikes in scattered geographic areas did little more than establish an IWW presence and style. Even the momentous 1912 victory at Lawrence failed to lead to permanent mass organizations in textiles. Dissatisfaction also arose from free speech fights which seemed to be deflecting the struggle against employers to one against municipalities. Following extensive discussion on these matters within the IWW press and at regional meetings, a new strategy was devised for use with harvest workers—the job delegate system. Under this schema, a small core of stationary organizers directed hundreds of mobile delegates who moved with the migratory workers. The delgates in the field were empowered to initiate new members, collect dues, and settle job disputes at the point of production. A local could exist in the hat or satchel of a mobile delegate.

The job delegate system was adopted by the IWW's Agricultural Workers Organization for the harvest of 1915. It was so effective that it was immediately used that autumn for lumber workers in the West where it proved to be even more successful. Funds generated by the harvest and lumber workers made new organizational drives possible in the Mesabi iron range and the copper fields of Montana and Arizona. Concurrent with these successes west of the Mississippi was the steady growth of the IWW in the Atlantic, Gulf and Great Lake ports. Dues paying membership leaped from 40,000 in 1916 to a peak of at least

100,000 in 1918. During various trials after 1917, the federal government put the IWW membership even higher, contending it had reached 250,000. This may have been an exaggeration to inflame fears of the IWW's power, but it also indicates a shrewd appraisal that many a worker who did not carry the red membership card or had not kept up dues payments was still to be counted a Wobbly.

The period of expansion involved a shift toward a more systematic trade unionism symbolized by the transfer of formal leadership in 1915 from Vincent St. John to William D. Haywood. "The Saint" had been important in shaping the characteristic attitudes of the IWW and had provided guidance for the first generation of IWW organizers. Son of a Wells Fargo pony express rider and schooled in bloody mine battles, St. John was much beloved by the IWW rank and file in the West. Rather than remaining active in daily IWW activities where he might come into conflict with the views now dominating the organization, the unassuming St. John went off to prospect for gold, promising to make a sizable donation to the IWW if he struck it rich.

While sharing St. John's Western origins and also having a father who had worked for Wells Fargo, Big Bill Haywood was an outgoing personality who had developed extensive contacts in the East and in Europe. Haywood came to the IWW after nearly twenty years experience as a nuts-and-bolts organizer for the Western Federation of Miners, and in 1907 he was the central figure in one of the the most sensational criminal trials of the day. Haywood was charged with being a party to the murder of Frank Steunenberg, former governor of Idaho, who after being elected with labor support had broken miners' strikes with troops. Eugene V. Debs announced in a special edition of *The Appeal To Reason* that if the employers succeded in what labor saw as a frameup, "a million revolutionists will meet them with guns." Clarence Darrow, the preeminent civil liberties attorney of the day, agreed to head the legal defense. By the time a verdict of not-guilty was reached, Haywood was so famous that vaudeville operators offered thousands of dollars a week if he would appear on their circuits. The six-foot miner who had lost an eye as a child turned them all down in favor of advancing radical causes. At one meeting in Chicago's Riverside Park organized by the Socialist Party, there were 60,000 paid admissions, and a Milwaukee audience numbered over 25,000.

Partly due to his celebrity status, Haywood was sent as an American delegate to the 1910 Congress of the Second International, convened in Copenhagen.[11] In the course of that trip, he met many prominent revolutionaries, trade unionists, and intellectuals. Among them were George Bernard Shaw, V.I. Lenin, Rosa Luxemburg, Ramsey MacDonald, Jean Jaurès and Clara Zetkin. Haywood addressed gatherings in Scandinavia and Great Britain, displaying an uncanny ability to strike the right tone wherever he went and whatever the class composition of his audience. He was a master of punchy ideological one-liners which served him well whether he was speaking before audiences with a limited grasp of English or being interviewed by the press. In the midst of the Lawrence textile strike, he posed the question of child labor memorably: "The worst thief is the one who steals the playtime of children." Asked to explain sabotage, he responded, "Sabotage means to push back, pull out or break off the fangs of capitalism." Characteristically, his autobiography begins by stating he derived no pleasure from knowing his ancestors were either Puritan bigots or pirates.

Quotable and charming as Haywood could be, he was also a no-nonsense organizer. By the time New Year's bells chimed in 1917, the IWW was thriving as never before. The one big union was firmly established among maritime, lumber, harvest and mine workers and, in other industries, had viable units that awaited funds and personnel to resume battle. Solid support for the IWW existed in the left wing of the Socialist Party, in ethnic federations, and in numerous AFL affiliates. More than a dozen daily papers in as many languages were being published, and efficiency was at an organizational all-time high. The establishment of strong and permanent industrial unions with a revolutionary perspective seemed within easy reach. The vista changed drastically in a matter of months.

PERSECUTION

Physical harassment had always been the lot of IWW organizers, and as the IWW grew more effective the violence directed against its members escalated. A symbolic turning point came in 1914 when Joe Hill was charged with the murder of two Salt Lake City grocers. The IWW felt this was a general warning for its organizers to get out of the land of the Mormons and a specific retaliation for Hill's parodies of religious hymns and his role in organizing Utah miners. A defense campaign which eventually won the support of President Wilson, the national AFL leadership and the Swedish Ambassador failed to save Joe Hill's life. In the succeeding years, murderous sheriffs and vigilantes added to the roll call of Wobbly martyrs. Brutal as these incidents were, they pale when compared to the systematic persecution of the IWW undertaken by the federal government in 1917.

As long as the IWW had floundered, its radicalism had been somewhat tolerable, and resistance to it had centered on local private enterprise. When the IWW began to prevail in some industries at a time when the war economy demanded a steady supply of basic raw materials and compliant labor, beleaguered employers called for federal intervention. They understood that only a national campaign could root out a decentralized organization like the IWW and that patriotic fervor could be used to facilitate their task. The stated aim of Woodrow Wilson's war policy was to "make the world safe for democracy." The unstated domestic byproduct was a war to make the economy safe for capitalism.

The opening phase of the federal assault came on September 7, 1917, when IWW halls were raided by federal officials and virtually every IWW leader was indicted for conspiracy to resist the war effort. These indictments named 166 Wobblies, including individuals such as Vincent St. John and Ben Williams, who were not presently active in the organization; Walter Nef, who was pro-war and pro-Ally; and Arturo Giovannitti, who was not even a formal member. Another of the indicted was on active duty in the army, and still another, Frank Little, was dead. The trials stemming from these indictments would effectively destroy the IWW infrastructure and end its threat both as a revolutionary organization and as a national trade union.

The plot against the IWW involved the Council on National Defense, the Attorney General, the Secretary of Labor, the Postmaster General, and President Wilson himself.[12] Also involved were numerous senators, judges, and military men. To guarantee enthusiastic public support for the government's campaign, the Justice Department sponsored the creation of the American Protective League as a vehicle for citizens anxious to combat subversion. In a little over a year, the American Protective League would grow to a membership of more than a quarter million with units in nearly a thousand cities and towns. Three million Americans would be cited by the League for "disloyalty."[13] Other "patriotic" organizations with names like the Liberty League, the Knights of Liberty, and the Home Defense League carried on similar witchhunts with a more regional focus.

The IWW had been uncharacteristically low-keyed about its opposition to World War I, especially after the U.S. became directly involved on April 19, 1917. The preponderant majority of Wobblies felt the war to be a purely capitalistic struggle for economic leverage that no worker should support. They agreed with

Haywood when he declared it was better to be a traitor to one's country than to one's class. Nonetheless, there was a consensus that once the nation was committed to war, opposition as an organization was suicidal. Refusal to be part of the war effort was left as a matter of individual conscience. Events soon demonstrated the government's objective in regard to the IWW was less to throttle anti-war sentiments than to jail the first, second, and third tier of its leadership. Individuals like St. John and Williams had to be included as they might come back to take the place of people like Haywood and Nef if the need arose. The inclusion of Frank Little, one of the most outspoken anti-war IWWs, may have been an error, as Little had been assassinated only a month before the indictments. Or Little may have been consciously included to lend credibility to the charge of a longstanding conspiracy.

At Haywood's urging, the IWW decided to meet the federal challenge head on. Instructions went out from national headquarters that all the indicted should turn themselves in and waive extradition rights. The IWW would agree to the government's plan for a mass trial in Chicago. Haywood's win-all or lose-all approach was based on the fact that the government's case was totally fabricated and that forces within the Wilson administration opposed the anti-IWW effort. George Vanderveer, the best and most experienced IWW attorney, would be available to handle the trial, and Vanderveer assured Haywood the case was legally theirs. The presence of sympathetic reporters like Carl Sandburg and John Reed guaranteed some favorable hearing in the press. The mass trial was a double-edged sword that Haywood thought he could appropriate to the advantage of industrial democracy. An acquittal would be a propagandistic thunderbolt of incalculable national impact.

Haywood's approach was opposed by Elizabeth Gurley Flynn, a nationally known IWW organizer who had come into serious conflict with him about legal defense strategy in a Mesabi Range miners' strike. She held that the longer legal proceedings took, the more likely the war hysteria would ebb, that the public needed as much time as possible to digest the hidden agenda behind the charges, and that any genuine dissent within the federal ranks could only fester as legal delays mounted. Flynn argued that each IWW should exercise every evasive and delaying tactic available, beginning with the evasion of warrants and fighting extradition. She and the three of the indicted who openly followed her advice—Carlo Tresca, Arturo Giovannitti and Joe Ettor—eventually had charges against them dropped. Those who followed Haywood's course were to be convicted and sentenced to prison terms of up to twenty years and fines of up to $20,000.

The convictions were devastating. One immediate consequence was that the IWW's limited resources were consumed in preparing appeals and raising bail. Precious years were consumed in these tasks, and then in April of 1921 when all appeals had been exhausted, rather than return to prison, Haywood and eight others among a group of forty-six free on bail elected to seek political sanctuary in the infant Soviet Union. Many IWWs were bitter that the "Big Guy" had deserted, particularly when he had been so adamant about the show-trial strategy. While there was sympathy for Haywood because of his failing health, his flight was more demoralizing than the immediate legal setbacks. When Haywood offered to return to the United States if the forfeited bail money would be returned to those who had posted it, the government would not come to terms with him. The government preferred a tarnished exile in Moscow to a steadfast hero in Leavenworth.

Had the IWW followed Flynn's strategy, it is unlikely the long term outcome would have been much different. The federal government was determined to destroy the IWW through a combination of direct assault and active support of state initiatives. Events in Wichita, Sacramento and Omaha demonstrated the kind of oppression the most nominal Wobbly might encounter. The Wichita IWWs had been involved in a campaign to organize Oklahoma and Kansas oil workers. An already virulent local anti-IWW campaign escalated in 1917, when U.S. District Attorney Fred W. Robertson arranged for a special session of the Kansas legislature to pass anti-IWW statutes. Robertson then instructed all federal attorneys in the state to jail *every* IWW in their jurisdiction. In Sacramento, the anti-IWW effort was marked by systematic disruption of the IWW defense committee. The committee treasurer was arrested fourteen times within a six-month period, and women volunteers were arrested on charges of prostitution. An attempt by the Wobblies to hold a conference on agriculture in Nebraska led to scores of IWWs being held for more than two years before charges were dropped. During this detention, as in many others, regular beatings by guards and horrendous prison conditions resulted in death, insanity, and chronic illness for many of the incarcerated.

Another disruptive aspect of the legal persecutions was a tragic quarrel within IWW ranks about whether jailed IWWs should accept pardons, which carried the legal implication of original guilt. An anti-clemency group that referred to IWW prisoners as "class war prisoners" argued that all releases should stem from the direct action of workers. Their opponents considered this position unrealistic and contrary to IWW precepts. The IWW never told workers what issues to strike over, and experience showed that most successful workplace disruptions were over direct exploitation of those involved, and not in support of distant battles, however worthy. The pro-clemency group felt the most important objective was to get Wobblies out of jail and back in action. Wobblies who accepted clemency as a means of getting early release were stunned when some IWWs who had never been in prison at all ostracized them as class traitors.

The IWW was not the only federal target. The mood of the anti-labor crusaders was summed up by Senator John Summers of Washington when he introduced a sedition bill aimed at stamping out "anarchy, sedition, disloyalty, IWWism, Bolshevism, radicalism, and un-Americanism in all their various forms."[14] Among the measures soon taken were banning radical literature from the mails, disrupting public meetings, denying Socialist officials posts to which they had been properly elected, and constant trials on a multitude of charges. Raids ordered by Attorney General Palmer in 1920 concentrated on ten thousand of the foreign born thought to be potential traitors.[15] Individual states provided crucial backup support by passing criminal syndicalist and sedition laws to jail dissidents whom the federal nets had missed.

The most flagrantly lawless element in the effort to dismantle the radical movement was the vigilanteeism tolerated at all levels of government. An infamous high point of such activity came in the lumber town of Centralia, Washington, in 1919. As preannounced by members of the American Legion, a Memorial Day Parade was transformed into a raid on the local IWW hall, a replay of previous assaults on other IWW halls and sympathizers in Centralia. This time, advised of their constitutional right to self-defense by their counsel, the IWWs resisted force with force. Before the defenders ran out of bullets, four of the invaders were dead. Revenge for these deaths came that very evening when a wounded Wesley Everest, the most militant of the IWW defenders, a returned war veteran, and the last to surrender, was taken from his cell by vigilantees. Everest was promptly castrated and lynched. Seven of the IWWs who had defended the hall were subsequently convicted of second degree murder and sentenced to terms of twenty-five to fifty years. No one was ever tried for the murder of Wesley Everest or for the attack on the IWW hall.

A significant number of IWWs perished in prison or served lengthy terms. Blackie Ford, charged with murder in a California harvest dispute in 1913, was not released until 1926. Six of the

Centralia defendents were not freed until 1933, while the seventh, Ray Becker, who held out for a full pardon, remained behind bars until 1940. Len De Caux, a Wobbly from 1921 to 1925 and later a CIO press chief and a member of the Communist Party, underscored the valor of the IWW rank and file when he wrote many years later:

> No major defectors took Judas money to turn against their cause. No pitiful string of renegades turned out to parrot propaganda of the class enemy, as happened during Cold War repression of the Left. The Wobbly working stiffs stood up and were counted. Most took it on the chin with exemplary loyalty to their class.[16]

Valid as this judgment is, the IWWs released from prison were not the same fighting force they had been prior to 1917. All had been fed on gruel for years. Many had been beaten regularly and some had been strapped to the bars of their cells for hours on end. Each had wondered how many of their prime years must be spent caged. The released radicals were physically and emotionally drained. With the possibility of revolution fading, they began to adjust their behavior to recalcitrant American realities and sought to enjoy some personal comforts. Their double bid for industrial unionism and socialist revolution had been brutally trumped by established economic and political power.

SCHISM AND DECLINE

Any chance for a revitalized IWW after the conclusion of World War I was destroyed by the formation of what came to be irreconcilable factions. These were not formal groups so much as tendencies which sometimes coalesced around a loose cluster of ideas. One tendency felt the solution to the IWW's problems was greater centralization and accountability, but among this group there was sharp disagreement about whether or not to merge with the developing Communist movement. The opposing tendency felt it was necessary for the IWW to have increased decentralization, with extremists calling for total local autonomy, no national dues, no central clearing house, and severe restrictions on the length and frequency that any individual could hold IWW office. The decentralizers also tended to be those most adamantly opposed to IWW prisoners accepting clemency.

The destructive nature of these disputes had an early manifestation in 1918, when the IWWs not caught up in the indictments of 1917 voted to make all former IWW leaders ineligible for future office. This effectively severed the organization from its own past, decapitating the IWW even more ruthlessly than the government had. Judgments of this type partly stemmed from inexperienced individuals suddenly taking the helm, but they also reflected the presence of *agents provocateurs*. Employers had a long history of placing spies within worker organizations, and the opportunities to promote discord in the midst of organizational chaos and constant persecution were numerous. When Haywood was released on bail and saw what was going on at national headquarters, he wandered about heartbroken and dazed.

The arguments and bad feelings among IWWs still free intensified when the final appeals on the federal convictions were lost. No group ever managed to command a majority, and the organization began to disintegrate. Individuals ceased paying dues, and functioning locals withdrew affiliation. The culmination of the internecine wrangling came in the disastrous convention of 1924 during which what remained of the organization cleaved in two. One group even went so far as to take out a legal injunction against the other regarding rights to property.

The remnant which eventually came to recognized as the official IWW became increasingly influenced by anarchist thinking, and after the formation of the CIO had to differentiate between CIO industrial unionism and IWW industrial unionism.[17] Indeed, as hopes of directly organizing masses of workers ebbed, the focus of the IWW swerved more toward educational work. Yet even with the organization in precipitous decline, a government once more led by a liberal Democrat placed the IWW on the subversive organizations list during the red scare following World War II. The IWW remained on that list for twenty years and the press cited any momentary IWW upsurge with alarm.[18] There was a flurry of interest in the IWW by the radicals of the 1960s, but by the early 1980s the circulation of the IWW newspaper, now a monthly, was approximately three thousand, with dues paying membership in the hundreds.

The Legacy

During the 1960s "The Ballad of Joe Hill," sung by social activist Joan Baez, won something of a mass audience and was extremely popular with campus radicals. One of the song's refrains states that Joe Hill, the IWW personified, never died. That apparently romantic sentiment contains far more truth than the conventional view that the IWW was a historic aberration. Many of the concepts and tactics pioneered by the IWW literally live on in organizations which often don't know their origins, just as numerous safety provisions won by the IWW remain in effect in mining, lumber and maritime operations.

Seen strictly as a trade union movement, the IWW was in the mainstream of American labor and for at least two decades was the central current of industrial unionism. Even more than the AFL, the IWW is the CIO's genuine historic link to nineteenth century predecessors. Conventional trade unionists often find this debt difficult to acknowledge because of the vast difference in the approach of reformist industrial unions. The reformists have abandoned a socialist perspective, and in place of direct action have substituted a labor bureaucracy parallel in form to that of management. Nothing illustrates this approach more vividly than the frequency with which national executive boards intervene in locals that elect radical leaders or present controversial agendas for national consideration. That this power is codified in laws that are clearly anti-labor in their intent is not coincidental.[19] Old-time Wobblies would not be surprised at the indifference so many workers display toward conventional unions or the steady erosion of labor's influence since the purge of labor radicals at the end of World War II.

No resurgence of the American labor movement is likely to occur without a revival of the IWW's insistence on the primacy of rank and file authority and, with that authority, responsibility. Without some prevision of the kind of worker-controlled economy projected by the IWW, powerful concepts like solidarity, direct action, civil disobedience, and even the general strike have no vitality. Organizing the unorganized remains an idle threat and marches on Washington harmless media events. Worker energy is forever forced into a cost of living race in which wages historically chase prices, while unions preoccupied with bureaucratic self-preservation cultivate established power. Labor becomes permanently locked into a defensive posture from which it reacts as best as circumstances allow to the vicissitudes of the capitalist economy. The Wobblies remind us that there was a time when many Americans did not accept the existence of giant corporations as essential for the economic welfare of the nation and did not assume a Tweedledee-Tweedledum two-party system was the best means of guaranteeing and extending democracy.

Just as the IWW's trade unionism has been eclipsed by reformist views, its revolutionary outlook has been eclipsed by the ideas of what may be called "the Class of 1917," those who believe some variation of the Bolshevik model of revolution is applicable to the United States. This view dominated American radical thinking until the 1960s and 1970s, when civil rights, anti-war, counter-cultural, environmental and women's rights advocates returned to practices in the tradition of the IWW. The French May of 1968 proved that the general strike remained a formidable weapon, and the formation of the Solidarity union in Poland demonstrated that the "one big union" seeking to reshape society nonviolently was more than a syndicalist specter. These domestic and international events suggest even the most ambitious political movements no longer have to be ideologically bound by hierarchical or militaristic models. An indigenous fount for mediating and alternate paths exists in the experience of the IWW and its historic antecedents.

Long regarded as belonging to a social movement whose time has come and gone, the IWW may yet prove to have been ahead of its time, developing and popularizing ideas very relevant to economic and political challenges undreamed of in 1905. Knowing that humans must always err, the IWWs dared to err on the side of liberty. The photographs we have gathered here show how that commitment to freedom blossomed into a profound mass movement. The words of rank and file IWWs that we present embody that sense of justice and reason which prompted ordinary workers to deeds of extraordinary courage.

—Dan Georgakas

INDUSTRIAL FREEDOM

I W W SONGS

To Fan
THE FLAMES of DISCONTE[NT]

Industrial Workers of the Worl[d]

10 CENTS Printed in U.[S.A.]

They had never heard the song before but with the instinct of the burdened they felt that this was their song, and that it was as closely allied to their strike, the first strike of their experience, as a hymn is allied to religion. They didn't know what the IWW was, what a labor organization meant, what class distinctions were. But the singing went straight to their hearts.
—B. Traven
The Cotton-Pickers

FANNING THE FLAMES

The Wobblies were a singing movement without peer in American labor history. IWWs sang as they picketed and paraded. They sang in jails and in the freight cars they called "rattlers." They sang at picnics and rallies, in saloons and hobo jungles. Singing was not a performance, but a community event in which everyone participated. An astonished news reporter observing the IWW-led Lawrence textile strike of 1912 commented, "It is the first strike I ever saw which sang. I shall not soon forget the curious lift, the strange sudden fire of the mingled nationalities at the strike meetings when they broke into the universal language of song."[1]

The most renowned IWW songsmiths were Swedish-born Joe Hill, a migrant worker with a genius for satire, and American-born Ralph Chaplin, a visual artist who also wrote moving poetry. Hill's "Casey Jones" and "The Preacher and the Slave" became part of the American folk music repertoire, and Chaplin's "Solidarity Forever" became the national anthem of labor. Among other IWW songwriters were Richard Brazier, Vera Moller, Charles Ashleigh,

• *Early edition of IWW songbook.*

Ethel Comer, Laura Payne Emerson and T-Bone Slim (Valentine Huhta). The IWW songwriters thought of their songs as expressions of working class ideals and tools to be used to better America. Any financial remuneration was channeled back to the IWW. Appropriately, popular IWW tunes like "Hallelujah, I'm a Bum!" and "I'm a Wandering Boy" were created anonymously and may have been group compositions.

The Little Red Song Book, provocatively subtitled, "IWW Songs to Fan the Flames of Discontent," was the closest thing the IWW had to a catechism. The first edition appeared in 1909, following the publication of a card of four songs in 1908. In the following seven decades there would be thirty-five separate editions featuring almost 200 different songs, with numerous printings per edition and uncounted translations. The songbook contained traditional labor songs, original compositions, and satiric parodies of popular tunes or church hymns. The selections shifted from edition to edition on the basis of an individual song's popularity and the availability of new material.

Closely allied with singing was story-telling and oratory. For decades Americans in pursuit of knowledge and entertainment had flocked to lecture halls and outdoor meetings. The Wobbly speakers were a brilliant last flowering of a tradition coming to an end with the introduction of the phonograph, motion pictures, and radio. The dynamic rhetorical style of the IWW fused the most dramatic speaking techniques then current with innovations designed for audiences not always fluent in English. Constant experimentation with mixed forms led to the inventive chalk talks of Red Doran and the one-man skits of Big Jim Thompson. Soapboxers also created or adapted various fables for use in public places. Most of this popular art has been lost, except where reproduced in fiction or recounted in oral histories.

IWW graphics proceeded from the same premises as IWW music. They ranged from large multi-colored posters to smaller handbills, mostly in black and white, to drawings, prints, and cartoons suitable for reproduction in periodicals. Distinctive and effective images presented unambiguous points of view, often with a sardonic or satiric twist. The highly inventive images were all the more remarkable in that most were created by people who never considered themselves professional artists and were widely displayed and appreciated by ordinary working people. Not the least among the IWW innovations were self-sticking labels which featured revolutionary symbols and slogans. Three millions of these "silent agitators" were printed in 1917 alone and mysteriously adhered themselves to walls all over America.[2]

I WILL WIN

SONGS

To Fan the Flames of Discontent

A distinguishing feature of the IWW approach was that rather than trying to win the allegiance of artists already recognized by the dominant culture, the IWW had the audacity to believe workers could create their own art. The aim was to liberate the imagination as well as the flesh. In the same way that the distance between leaders and members was consciously minimized, the IWW reduced the conventional gulf between artist and audience. IWW art was truly of, by, and for fellow workers. IWW posters were for street display, not for the gallery or museum. IWW literature was to be recited aloud, not read silently. IWW songs, jokes, and parables were to enter public consciousness as mass entertainment.

Like the ideal of industrial democracy itself, IWW art addressed immediate issues without forsaking a visionary perspective. Richard Brazier, contributor of sixteen songs to the first IWW song book, believed there were many reasons why IWWs loved to roam the West: "In addition to searching for the job, we were looking for something to satisfy our emotional desire for grandeur and beauty."[3] In a 1925 issue of *Industrial Solidarity*, prolific IWW author Covington Hall denounced those who would be friends of priesthoods while denouncing the prophet and dreamer, "who thinks outside of things as they are, ahead of the herd, beyond tomorrow. Yet in their sacred hearts, all men and women are always dreaming, are always visioning things that are not, but should be, and this we must do or perish."[4]

Militant songs became firmly established as part of trade unionism and reached heights comparable to the IWW's in the late 1930s. But not until the 1960s were there social movements that had the total cultural approach characteristic of the IWW. Most prominent among those actively carrying forward a specific IWW singing and storytelling tradition was Bruce "Utah" Phillips. Belonging to a much younger generation of Wobblies than the other voices presented in this book, Phillips sings and tells stories both in concert hall formats and on picket lines. His "Larimer Street" was included in the edition of the song book published on May 1, 1973. Utah Phillips says of himself: "I sing songs about trains, coal mines, unions, factories, working people, lazy people, the old and new West, bums, politicians, and the different things that happen to you when you're in love. And I tell stories and try to get people laughing and singing together. You know most of the songs I sing really belong to those people—they just don't know it yet."[5]

Bruce "Utah" Phillips

Most people I meet know some of the IWW songs even if they do not know their origin. We had terrific song writers like Ralph Chaplin, Richard Brazier, Joe Hill, and T-Bone Slim. Their songs are very, very simple. I've often been criticized for singing them by left-wing people who say they are too simplistic. Well, the songs were to help people define their problems and to suggest what the solutions might be. A lot of working folks came from other countries and couldn't speak very much English and didn't have a chance to go to school here. If the songs were going to communicate, they had to be simple. Our protest music of today tends to be a little more abstract. It's harder to understand. There's a lot of difference between, "How many miles must a white dove sail before it can rest in the sand?" and "Dump the bosses off your back."

We liked to steal the old Christian hymns because everyone knew the tune. We just changed the words so they made more sense. New verses got written all the time. The Wobblies would also take a popular tune and change the words. T-Bone Slim, the giant logger who spent a lot of his life in Kentucky working with Aunt Molly Jackson, was good at that. I believe he died in New York working on a tugboat. Anyway, one of his best songs was a parody of "They Go Wild, Simply Wild, Over Me." He called it "The Popular Wobbly." It goes like this:

I'm as mild-mannered man as can be,
And I've never done them harm that I can see;
Still on me they put a ban, they threw me in the can,
They go wild, simply wild over me.
　　They accuse me of ras-cal-i-ty,
　　But I can't see why they always pick on me;
　　I'm as gentle as a lamb, but they take me for a ram,
　　They go wild, simply wild over me.
Oh, the "bull" he went wild over me,
And he held his gun where everyone could see;
He was breathing rather hard when he saw my union card,
He went wild, simply wild over me.

• Drawing by Joe Hill.

Songs were used to teach basic IWW principles. They might express our position against craft unions. The IWW has always believed that there is an essential solidarity in the entire working class and that anyone who works for wages, whether a college professor or a ditch digger, is in the working class. We advocate that all the skilled, semi-skilled, and unskilled workers of the world band together in one giant, humongous union, the OBU, the "One Big Union." Instead of having a hundred little strikes settled, you could have a general strike that could take the system apart and then put it back together so that it made more sense. You would have the tools of production in the hands of the producers. You would start creating for use rather than for profit, abundance for the workers and nothing for parasites. Richard Brazier wrote "The Four Hour Day" to the tune of "Old Black Joe" to give a sense of what might be. The last verse and chorus sum up the message:

Now workingmen, we are working far too long;
That's why we've got this vast unemployed throng.
Give every worker a chance to work each day;
Let's join together and to the boss all say:

We're going to take a four hour day.
We surely will surprise the boss some First of May.

Earlier in this century the migratory worker used the freight train, old dirty face, to commute to the job. In the Northwest you'd come into a town and find a whole street loaded with people called "labor sharks." They would tell you what mine field or logging camp was hiring and you paid for a job, but they sold that one job as often as they could. You'd wind up with five hundred people showing up for fifty jobs. The IWW in Spokane decided that had to stop. They wanted a union hiring hall where you didn't have to pay for your jobs and where you had some control over working conditions. The bosses hated that so they tried to close down the hall by impounding the records and stopping publication of our paper. The IWW took to the streets and started soapboxing across from where the "Starvation Army" was set up, bible banging and Jesus preaching. The IWW had to be stopped, so the bosses had the city pass an ordinance against speaking in the streets, which, of course, was against the First Amendment of the Constitution. Word was spread over the Northwest and all along the coast that anybody cut loose from a job was to come to Spokane, Washington. That was the great Free Speech Fight of 1910. The fellow workers came in from everywhere, even old Scandinavian and Finnish miners who didn't speak very much English. They filled up the city and county jails, filled up Fort Wright, filled up the high school gymnasium, the Coliseum. Taxpayers started to bitch about these people they were feeding. The ordinance had to be changed. That's called the tactics of direct action, and they come to you highly recommended.

One of the songs for the Spokane Free Speech Fight was composed by Joe Hill and was introduced to the streets by Haywire McClintock, a well-known singer very active in the IWW in those parts. Haywire would hide in a doorway with T-Bone Slim. They had a tube and a garbage can lid for percussion and a guitar. A mass of workers would be gathered around the Starvation Army donut dollies. A man would walk by carrying an umbrella and a briefcase and dressed in a tight suit with a string tie and a bowler hat. He looked just like a banker, but functioned like a carny shill. He'd yell, "I've been robbed! I've been robbed! Help, I've been robbed!" Everyone would rush over to him. "What's the matter, what's the matter?" they'd ask. When enough had crowded around, he'd shout, "I've been robbed by the capitalist system!" And then the boys would jump out from the doorway and start singing Joe Hill's song:

Long-haired preachers come out every night,
Try to tell you what's wrong and what's right;
But when asked how 'bout something to eat,
They will answer with voices so sweet:

　You will eat, bye and bye,
　In that glorious land above the sky:
　Work and pray, live on hay,
　You'll get pie in the sky when you die.

That would go for two more verses with the chorus repeated and then it would end:

Workingmen of all countries unite;
Side by side we for freedom will fight.
When the world and its wealth we have gained
To the grafters we'll sing this refrain:

　You will eat, bye and bye,
　When you've learned how to cook and to fry;
　Chop some wood, t'will do you good,
　And you'll eat in the sweet bye and bye.

● *Painting by IWW R.D. Ginther.*

*. . .in the harvest fields that summer,
my real education, as opposed to that
of the academe, continued. These
Wobblies, knights of the road, as
they jocularly called themselves,
set me to thinking as no professor
had that first year in college.*
—William L. Shirer
Twentieth Century Journal

BINDLESTIFFS

In pre-World War I America, the itinerant workforce numbered in the millions. Poorly paid and treated harshly by employers, the migrant workers, usually males in their teens and twenties, drifted from one temporary job to another, often shifting from agricultural work to jobs in lumber, mining, or construction and usually ending a work year as penniless as when they began. Called "bindlestiffs" or "blanketstiffs" because of the small bundle of worldly goods they carried over their shoulders from job to job, the itinerants seemed much too mobile and heterogeneous a workforce to ever be organized. But the IWW, refusing to abandon any group of workers, struggled for years to find ways to reach itinerants in some systematic manner and enforce industry-wide wage and work demands on literally thousands of employers. By the early teens, after developing the job-delegate system in various lumbering and agricultural drives, IWW organizers decided to concentrate their efforts on harvest workers in the Midwest.

The new IWW organizing vehicle created in Kansas City before the harvest of 1915 was named the Agricultural Workers Organization 400 (AWO). This "one big agricultural union" sought to limit hours of work, improve wages, win free transportation on freight trains, provide relief from the caprices of local governments, and replace individual job-by-job arrangements with

• *Bindlestiff "jungle."*

collective bargaining. During the first year of its existence, the AWO enrolled 3,000 members. In 1917 and 1918, with some 300 mobile delegates in the field, membership swelled to 20,000 and then a disputed high of 50,000. The dues collected by the AWO invigorated the entire IWW. Of the total organizational income of $49,000 in 1916, fully a third came from the harvest workers. From that time on to the schism of 1924, the AWO always accounted for between one-third to one-half of annual IWW dues income.

Much as hard times had worked against the IWW during the first years of its existence, IWW growth in agriculture after 1915 was partly fed by the rise in agricultural prices brought on by the war in Europe. Farmers were able to grant benefits with little, if any, loss in total profit. Decades later some former Wobbly activists speculated that the organization might have been wiser if it had used this relatively prosperous time to concentrate on the family-oriented workers in basic industries. Their views were partly influenced by the judgment that the AWO was doomed to stagnate because of the mechanization of the harvest process, which would be most momentous in the very regions the AWO was most powerful. This evaluation minimizes the continuing importance of harvest workers in other regions and the ability of the IWW to improvise new tactics for new conditions.[1]

Whatever the long term prognosis might have been had the IWW survived the 1920s as a dynamic organization, the success of the AWO in 1915 opened a new era for the One Big Union. Never before had the IWW succeeded in organizing so many workers over so vast a geographic area. Funds generated by the harvest workers allowed the IWW, for the first time in its history, to carry on simultaneous, decently financed drives in timber, mining and agriculture. The victories that followed in the Pacific Northwest were directly linked to the impact of AWO funds, organizers trained in the harvest fields, and the application of the job delegate system.

By the end of its second year of existence, the AWO could raise the demand that all hiring be done either through IWW halls or IWW delegates on the job site. *De facto* picket lines stretched hundreds and hundreds of miles, for any would-be harvest hand without a red card was likely to be ejected from freight cars by IWW militants. Some Wobblies objected to such rough-house methods, but the consensus was that workers without an IWW card were really scabs. Preventing strikebreakers from ever reaching the job seemed more prudent than trying to deal with them at the point of production, where a sheriff could offer

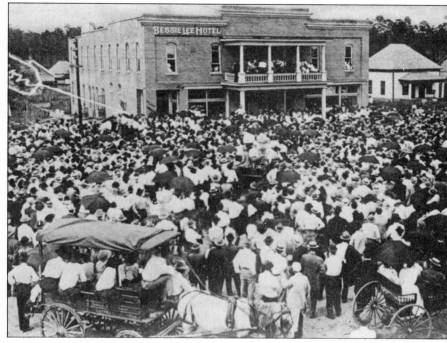

• *A.L. Emerson addresses 5,000 Louisiana timber workers, 1911.*

protection. How the Wobblies felt about scabs was expressed in a description attributed to Jack London that was reprinted in the song book, newspapers, and other IWW literature. Five blistering paragraphs began:

> After God had finished the rattlesnake, the toad, and the vampire, he had some awful substance left with which to make a SCAB. A SCAB is a two-legged animal with a corkscrew soul, a water-logged brain, and a combination backbone made of jelly and glue. Where others have hearts, he carries a tumor of rotten principles.

Among potential scab forces available to agricultural bosses were southern blacks. Prior to the harvest of 1916, the threat was raised that 30,000 black workers would be recruited in the rural South and brought directly to the harvest fields to crush the AWO. Far from being intimidated by the threat of imported black strikebreakers, the IWW newspapers responded with glee:

The IWW has some good Negro organizers, just itching
for a chance of this kind. Thirty thousand Negroes will
come and 30,000 IWWs will go back. The red card is
cherished as much by and its objectives understood as
well by a *black* man as a white.[2]

The editorials were not bravura posturing. In the years directly
preceding the formation of the AWO, the IWW had been involved
with the racially integrated Brotherhood of Timber Workers
(BTW), a union which grew to a peak membership of 35,000,
mainly concentrated in lumbering areas of Texas and Louisiana.
The first unit of the BTW was organized in 1910 by ninety
Louisiana workers sympathetic to the IWW and the Socialist Party.
Led by Arthur L. Emerson and Jay Smith, two whites, the union
understood that, since half of the lumber workers in the South
were black, successful organization without black participation
was impossible. Following the practice of earlier southern unions,
each local had a separate unit or lodge for each race. But the
Brotherhood was very cautious in its public statements, aware that
a union tolerating any black members, whatever the terms of
affiliation, would be doubly offensive to the racist and anti-union
mores of the South. Despite its name, the organization also
accepted women as full members, yet another affront to
conventional sensibilities in the region.

The initial practical link between the BTW and the IWW was
Covington Hall, a New Orleans-based IWW organizer and writer
who did publicity work for the Brotherhood. Formal unity came
in 1912 following a trip by Bill Haywood which became truly
historic when he successfully argued for totally integrated seating
arrangements at his unity meetings in Alexandria, Louisiana. That
autumn, D.R. Gordon, a black member of the BTW, was one of
the delegates to the IWW national convention. Despite a
temporary uplift provided by its affiliation with the IWW, the
Brotherhood was unable to hold off the legal and physical assault
of the Southern Lumber Operators Association and was shattered
before the AWO came into existence. The men who controlled the
economy of the South were not about to give the resurgent IWW
a second chance to revolutionize 30,000 agricultural workers
whose grievances ran even deeper than those of the lowliest white
itinerants. Their threat to mobilize black scabs never materialized.

Not all farmers were hostile to the IWW. The Non-Partisan
League, with roots in the old Populist movement, advocated a
socialist economy, and its members believed that they and their

employees could make common cause against bankers, railroad magnates, and industrial capitalists. In 1917, the League volunteered to negotiate wages, hours and conditions. Prevented by IWW policy from entering a written contract, the AWO announced "understandings" which were generally accepted as binding by Non-Partisan League farmers and their hired help.

Bindlestiffs had been critical to the development of the IWW long before they formed the AWO. A group of twenty migrants styling themselves the "Overalls Brigade" had played a crucial role in the debate which established direct action as the guiding principle of the organization. Clad in black shirts, denim overalls, and red kerchiefs, the Overalls Brigade led by "General" John J. Walsh held scores of public meetings at various Wobbly strongpoints along the long freight route from their home base in Portland to Chicago, the 1908 convention site. The enthusiasm they generated for direct action provided the momentum for the defeat of the political actionists. This particular group issued the first IWW song cards and sometimes argued that songs were the only propaganda the organization required. Bindlestiffs also took the lead in the free speech fights, frequently expressing the feeling that since they had no families to support they could take more chances than other workers.

Although the actual behavior of the migratory workers who advocated direct action most often amounted to what is usually termed a "slowdown" or "working to book," one would have to be naive to imagine that the everyday violence of the freight trains and workplaces never became part of a worker's defense of a job or bid for increased benefits. Just how complex the issue of violence became is evident in the experiences of IWW bindlestiffs Jack Miller and Joe Murphy. The men sometimes seem to be describing different organizations. Apart from individual personality traits, this phenomenon is largely accounted for by the circumstance that they are describing different phases of IWW history.

Jack Miller concentrates on 1914 to 1916, when the AWO was in ascendancy and the prospects for the triumph of industrial unions seemed bright. Like many of the migratory workers, Miller worked in lumber as well as in the harvest fields, and his recounting of the more bitter struggles of the Northwest is included in another section of this book.

Joe Murphy's focus is the early 1920s. He brags that he was born in the same year as the IWW. This would have made him 16 years old in 1921. By this time Joe Hill, Frank Little and Wesley Everest had been martyred; Haywood and seven others had chosen exile in the Soviet Union; and thousands of Wobblies were locked up in state and federal prisons. These factors intensified the already violent and coercive nature of the work environment of the mobile workers who made up the bulk of IWW membership in the West, but Murphy's two-fisted response was typical of many Westerners who had been in the IWW from the start. Murphy remained active in the labor movement throughout his life, enjoying a long career in the building trades unions until blacklisted in the 1950s.

Jack Miller

West of the Mississippi was the migrant worker. No matter what job was offered, he would say he could do it and let the boss find out whether or not that was true. The migratory workers were the most versatile body of men that ever developed on this continent. A tunnel had to dug, a bridge built, a dam constructed. The word went out and the workers with various skills would respond. The painters, riggers, mechanics, printers, teamsters—any trade you name—would arrive at the job by boxcar. They cut timber and harvested every major grain: wheat, oats, barley, and rye.

The Agricultural Workers Organization 400 brought a revolution to the harvest fields. Their headquarters was in Minneapolis and the secretary was Walter Nef. The jurisdiction of the AWO wasn't just the environs of Minneapolis. They intended to organize every harvest worker from Wisconsin to the Rockies, as far north and as far south as they could go. The immediate demand was four dollars pay for ten hours work. That was the first time farmers ever heard of limitation of hours. The idea was that employers would not be going face-to-face with individuals, but with an organization.

Harvest work was not easy. Working on the header barges, the wagons that hauled the grain, was so hard you never saw any fat men. On some of the other jobs, a teamster might have to control forty mules at a time. And the weather could get very hot. I was in Lincoln Center, Kansas, one year, and for a period the temperature hit over 110 degrees for ten days straight. I saw five men go down with heat exhaustion in a single day, and the boss was out for two weeks. But we had to do the harvest. Wheat does not wait. There is a period when it is ripe enough to cut. After that, the hull opens and the wheat falls on the ground. That's nature's provision for reproduction. The way it worked out was that we were unwanted until a few days before the harvest, and when it was over we got booted out as fast as possible. The AWO was putting an end to all that. I had been a member of the Socialist Party of America previously and had taken part in the Minot Free Speech Fight in 1913. I tried to join the IWW in 1914, but I could never catch up with anyone with cards until almost two years later. By then the harvest workers were flocking to the IWW by the thousands. In 1916, the membership of the AWO had tripled.

In those days, everyone treated the harvest stiff badly. One time in Council Bluffs, I and five traveling companions were waiting in a flat car when the head brakeman came through trying to collect fares before the train got started. He wanted fifty cents to carry us to Missoura Valley. I told him if he wanted to stay healthy, he should do the job he was paid for and not worry about taking fares. I was skinny enough to haunt a house at that time and he was huge, so he just took a swing at me with his brake stick, one of those gadgets they put through the spokes of the little wheels on top to lighten up the brake chains. I was expecting that and ducked. I was able to move fast, wrench it from his hand, and toss it across the tracks into a swamp.

He took off towards the caboose, and in a short time he had the whole train crew of twenty with him. I told my companions we'd have big trouble unless I could make it a personal thing. I told them not to interfere as the crewmen had us outnumbered. He had another brake stick and was making dire threats. I told him he was big, ugly, mean, dirty and strong but that he lacked guts. I picked up five rocks from the trainbed and told him, "Listen Billy, I've taken one brake stick from you and don't want to take another. Let's make it you and me with no weapons." He threw down his stick and I dropped the rocks. The only thing in my favor was that I had tried to be a wrestler once and knew some tricks. I understood that I could never knock him out with one punch and I could never sustain his weight. My best chance was to catch

• *Lunch break on Minnesota farm, 1911.*

him in a hip lock and roll him down into the swamp. There was enough mud there so that his strength wouldn't count. That's just how it worked out. I was able to keep his face in the swamp water until his eyes dilated and I knew he was too weak to do me any harm. I had won over his friends on the bank. They yelled, "Don't drown him, Slim. Get him up here and kick the hell out of him. Put the boot to him." I found out later he was the champion bully of this division, and here a little hundred and twenty pounder had taken him. The hoghead, that's the engineer, told me I could ride to wherever I wanted to go in his cab. I told him it was too small for six men. We'd wait for the next train.

A few days later when we got to Mitchell there was about two hundred people in the jungle. They had heard about the fight and passed a motion that our group should stay behind to try to organize the railroad workers. I hadn't been an official member for but ten days, and I didn't have anything but agriculture literature and some song books. I didn't even know the roundhouse lingo. Just the the same, we respected the will of the majority. If they wanted us to organize the railroad men, that's what we would do. It turned out the company had some people waiting for us at the depot, so we were not successful.

The IWW was branded as violent. People misunderstood our use of words like *sabotage* and *direct action*. Most often, it is said that *sabotage* comes from the French word *sabot*, the word for the wooden shoe that workers tossed into their machines when they got fed up. I'm told that isn't the true origin of the word, but what I am very sure about is that we didn't use that kind of sabotage. We did not burn down sawmills. What's the use of burning down your source of employment? No, sabotage meant the conscious withdrawal of efficiency. You might be working on a threshing machine. If you threw up the bundles fast and in a certain way, there would be a lot of waste. Teeth in the machine might get broken off and the stacker could get clogged. The farmer saw that he would get less wheat in twelve hours than he could get in eight if we were working with more efficiency.

We never felt as badly toward the farmer as toward some of the other types of boss. Our songs showed him as more of a caricature than a villian. Often he might be oppressed by the same things that oppressed us. We had to fight him, but sometimes we felt sorry for him. He was determined to have it his way. It was his machine and his wheat; but it was our bodies and our time. We never did physical harm to anyone with our sabotage. If the farmer is disabled, the job stops. We were there to work and earn wages, not to destroy. If I saw a man put a box of matches to a sheaf of wheat, I'd wrap a pitchfork handle around his neck. Don't take the Joe Hill songs about the farmer too literally. Joe Hill was a poet. We understood that.

All direct action means is dealing directly with the boss. If you want to shorten it, direct action means you gain all your objectives on the job rather than through the ballot box. That idea got misrepresented as sabotage. You could use direct action anywhere, even in jail. In Minot, during the Free Speech period, they put a bunch of IWWs on the rock pile and told them to break rocks. They broke one big one and passed the pieces around as souvenirs. Then they broke the handles off the sledges and threw them over the fence. That ended the rock breaking.

The term bullpen came from the Minot struggle too. They were arresting us so fast that the jail couldn't hold all the prisoners. They built a stockade next to the jail, like the one for bulls who were to be shipped out. Afterwards they got to calling all general receiving tanks in a jail the *bullpen*. Then it got transferred to mean any cell.

If it had not been for my contact with the IWW and what I gained from them, I would have probably become a criminal. I mean a real criminal. Like many migratory workers, I had left the mill of religion behind me. I couldn't even be threatened with hell. I had no respect for institutions, because I saw how they worked. I had no way to evolve a sense of values that would make me a social being. I was rebellious. If an indignity was heaped on me, I would think of means of retaliation. I would perhaps have killed a police officer who was unjustly trying to arrest me, because I would not be intimidated. I would have been dead long since— the unknown and unsung criminal I was meant to be.

Through the IWW I began to consider how man had risen from the beastly stage through the ages. I could see a future that I could be part of creating. I began to see how you contribute to my well-being and I to yours. I saw what love was in the finest sense. If it were not for the IWW I would not use the language I am now using. I would still speak in the workingman's lingo as an uneducated person. The IWW sparked the imagination. We said, "What force on earth is weaker than the feeble strength of one?" I used the Aesop fable about a bundle of sticks. Two men united do not double their strength, they quadruple it. If the numbers are sufficient, workers can dictate the terms of living. We fought for material gains like beans, clothing, and schooling, but we had a much larger vision. We were not making a new building in the shell of the old, not a new city, not a new country—we were building a new world. What greater task, what greater inspiration could there be than that we workers were the only ones who could do this? It would be enough just to save this world, but we were going to build another and better one. That's still true. Unless working people take hold, our species will pass out in an atomic holocaust or we will starve or smother to death in air unfit to breathe.

Joseph Murphy

My father was one of the organizers of the American Railway Union. By the time I was born in San Francisco, he had been blacklisted all over the country. Eventually he ended up back in Springfield, Missouri, his home town, where he became a yardmaster, but when I was very young, he was blacklisted. In order for him to get from division to division of the railroad, he'd have to wait for a union conductor to come on duty. I have letters in my possession which indicate that the password was "Hot Springs." Well, there were six boys and six girls in the Murphy family that were traveling to "Hot Springs," Arkansas. The union conductors would move us from division to division, and sometimes they'd even take us home for a meal.

I first heard of the IWW through my brother Emmet. He ran away from home when he was a kid and joined the IWW. The Missouri papers of that time billed the IWW as a bunch of devils who were out to sabotage the world. The truth is that the IWW did practice sabotage to a certain extent.

Let's take the example of farmers. They liked to pay us off with pickhandles instead of money, and if a worker took the case to a labor commission, if there was a labor commission, it would take thirty days for a hearing. So the worker had to use sabotage to put the fear of Jesus into John Farmer. That's what they did, either by burning wheat fields or barns or some other act. John Farmer wanted you to work twelve hours a day, and we wanted to work for ten hours a day. John wanted us to work for forty cents an hour and we wanted fifty cents. In John Farmer was the worst vestige of feudalism in America. John always had extra work for you: go out and milk the cow or unharness the horses or curry the mules. The vast majority of food he served was from the frying pan: fried ham, fried chicken, fried steak; and it was always burned to pieces.

The worst food was served by a California outfit, Miller and Lux, one of the largest hirers of agricultural workers. They paid a dollar a day for twelve hours work. Their food was rotten, but they were so afraid the bindlestiffs would carry off the plates that they nailed the plates to the tables and washed them off with a hose after we got through eating. That was the only washing the plates ever got. We called Miller and Lux the dirty plate crowd.

In Kansas it was better. We got fed five times a day by the German farmers because they knew you had to eat in order to produce. This was before the combines came in, so we would shuck wheat mostly or else pitch it into the harvester. The heat was up over 110 degrees in the sun. We would look across the plains and see a freight train miles away and think of moving on. The water was alkaline, and it gave you diarrhea or dysentery. The farmers became accustomed to it, but it took an awful long time for outsiders to be comfortable.

We had a poem about how to resist John Farmer. Actually I would call it doggerel:

> If freedom's road seems rough and hard
>   and strewn with rocks and thorns,
> Just put your wooden shoes on pard,
>   and you won't hurt your corns.

That reminded us that although organizing and teaching was a very good way of persuading people, you could not get along without the help of the good old wooden shoe. By that we meant the *sabot*, the French word for the wooden shoe the farmers wore. When one of the workers wanted to rest, he'd toss his *sabot* into the machinery and it would break down. That's where the word *sabotage* came from. So the wooden shoe was the symbol of that, and so was the black cat. They were our emblems of sabotage.

I first joined the IWW in June of 1919. I had run away from home before to go to the strawberry harvest in Arkansas. This time, when I was fourteen, I joined the wheat harvest and encountered Wobblies who were attempting to hold out for fifty cents an hour and ten hours a day.

You have to remember the situation we were up against. In California, the ranchers and big business had put through a criminal syndicalism law that meant that membership in the IWW more or less made you an outlaw. One story we told was that after a fellow had taken out a card in California, he asked the organizer what his card entitled him to. The organizer said, "If they catch you with it, it entitles you to two to fourteen in San Quentin or Fulsom." The laws were enacted to keep us from organizing agricultural workers.

One of the big advantages of being in the IWW at that time was being able to ride the freight trains. Riding a freight car was miserable, but it was the only way a migratory worker could go

from job to job or seek a job in the harvest. The Wobblies used physical force to unload riders who didn't have a red card. Then the railroaders got so they would unload riders who didn't have a red card too. A lot of men took out a card just to ride the trains. I think now that one of the mistakes we made was to spend too much time trying to organize the riffraff instead of the home guard, the guys who stayed in one place. We would have built a more substantial organization by concentrating on the home guard instead of the ones that just took out a card to ride the freight trains. We made men out of many of them on skid row, but when you have proletarian riffraff—as Marxists called them, the *lumpenproletariat*—you got an awful low life form to organize.

I became a delegate in the harvest about September when they gave me what we call the *rigging*. We were fighting to keep our places on trains. In those days, there were petty racketeers who would come along the edge: the fireman, the engineer, two brakemen, and a conductor. They would have pick handles in their hands, and they would make everybody donate either a dollar or a pocket watch or a pocket knife. The Wobblies put a stop to that. We beat the hell out of a few dozen train crews. They got the message real quick that they weren't going to shake us down just to ride their trains.

There's nothing more discouraging than to ride a boxcar for eight to twelve hours between one division and another, hungry, cold, wet, lousy, and then look out across the country and see the lights in a house with people gathered around a table. The only home you have is in the insides of a boxcar or maybe a gondola—a gondola is an open car that hauls sand and coal—and you're all wet and look at this beautiful light in the distance or even close by as you roll along or wait for another train to pass.

One story we told goes like this: There was a little girl who went to the door and a harvest hand, a Wobbly, was at the door asking for some work to do in order to get something to eat. She said, "Mama, there's a bum at the door," and Mama answered, "That isn't a bum; that's a harvest worker." A month later, the harvest was over and the same Wobbly was at the door rapping for some work and the little girl says, "Mama, there's a harvest worker at the door," and Mama replies, "That's no harvest worker; that's a bum."

We told stories like that to amuse ourselves. You see the IWW had a sense of humor, which the other radical organizations never did. Different groups were different, too. The Finns, for example, were very serious. If you spoke before a group of Finns, they were reserved. They'd never laugh. You could tell your best joke and it would be wasted. It was too serious a proposition for them. The Communist Party and the Socialist Party and the Socialist Labor Party were like that. I think that's because they were mainly made up of petty bourgeois.

What I was talking about was the dirty, miserable existence on the freight trains. You'd get lousy very easily in the empty boxcars from the paper when you'd lie down, because so many of the men were dirty and wouldn't boil up. *Boiling up* meant taking a five gallon can and filling it with water and putting in your clothes and building a good fire underneath it in order to keep clean. The Wobblies preached that cleanliness was next to godliness, in order to get members to stay clean.

Freight traveling was something you had to do, not something you wanted to do. Then for a time it got real dangerous, because hijacks tried to take over. It was 1922 and I was elected to the Flying Squad which was assigned to take care of the hijacks. The hijacks worked like this: Generally there were three or four of them, armed with .38s and .45s, but mostly .38s. They'd stick up a hundred harvest hands in a boxcar. They had a rope ladder that they came down over the top with, and if somebody got a little smart with them they'd give them a little push and the train would be going thirty or forty miles an hour and the guy would fall under the train and be ground to bits. This was known as *greasing the rails*, and was quite common.

There's only one way to deal with that stuff. We took them hijacks, many of them; we took a razor, a Gem razor blade, and cut "IWW" on their face, "I" on the forehead and "W" on each cheek. Then we put permanganate potassium into it. That marked them up. We got a surprise out in Spokane, Washington. A group of hijacks had been sticking up apple workers. Two or three days after we got to them, an article came out in the Spokane paper that the IWW had marked up one of their cops. He was one of them hijacks.

We did away with some other types too. We did away with the gamblers, the tin-horn gamblers and the D-horns, the ones that peddled canned heat and cheap wine and beer. We said that the D-horn's nose was deepest red, a parody on "The Red Flag" to educate members not to do any drinking. Personally, I've more than made up for it since.

Working conditions were very important to us. In 1924, we were building a dam and a tunnel for the city of Seattle to get water and power projects for the county. The guys who were working in the glory hole, the glory hole was where they were going to build the dam, were getting it bad. The builders were such a highball outfit that they insisted that every skiff be loaded over the top. The result was that stones kept falling off and hitting the workers in the glory hole. The tunnel work was just as bad. They would run men in just after they'd shot dynamite, and the workers would catch gas. They would get terrific headaches from that.

So we were on strike against those conditions, and we put in for more money too. After a while, they started shipping in scabs. We found out that the scabs were being hired in Minneapolis, so a bunch of us beat our way back to the employment agency that was shipping them and signed on. As soon as they put us on the train back to Washington, we started to unload all the first class scabs. There were some guys who said they would go along with whatever we did. So we just let the company take us across the country until we got back to Town Creek, Washington. They took us off the train and put us on buses to go up to the tunnel. As we came up on the site, we started to sing:

> Hold the fort for we are coming;
> Union men be strong.
> Side by side, we battle onward;
> Victory will come.

That really pissed them off. They had fed us, wined and dined us, all the way from Minnesota, thinking we were scabs, and all the time we were a bunch of Wobblies.

Sometimes it got a lot more violent. In 1919, it was Centralia. I had been in the harvest from Kansas to Canada and had come into Washington to pick apples. It was the night of November 11th in Seattle when the message came to the hall that the American Legion had raided our hall in Centralia. About a hundred of us took the big G, the Great Northern, to Centralia, where we were met by about a thousand Legionnaires and company gunmen. They had raided the hall that day. When they broke in, four Legionnaires had been killed, and they had captured about ten Wobblies and thrown them in the can. Supposedly, only one Wobbly was lynched that night, Wesley Everest, but three or four others were taken out and we never saw them again. A doctor told an Elks meeting one night that Wesley Everest had been castrated before he was lynched.

At the Centralia trial, eight Wobblies were found guilty. Members of the American Legion went into the courts and were paid three dollars a day by the lumber barons to intimidate the jury. Any worker that showed up was either put out of town or given thirty days. I was given thirty days because I had on a sack shirt and they found my rigging. The convicted Wobblies were given twenty-five to forty-five years in Walla Walla Penitentiary. Later, the jury said they were intimidated by the Legionnaires with their uniforms, and they all signed affidavits to that effect throughout the years to get our guys released. There is a monument in Centralia to the four Legionnaires that were killed. I'd donate money to see it blown off the map.

Centralia was a very emotional part of my life. It made me hate the employing class more than ever. The morning when Elmer Smith was brought back to jail to gather his blankets up—in those days you had to have blankets in jail too—he turned to the eight of them that had been found guilty and said, "Just remember, fellas, I've got a few dollars and my brother's got a few dollars, so as long as we have any money, I'll continue to fight for you to get you out." Which he did, until the day he died. We were up in Yakima, Washington, myself and another Wobbly, when the waitress, I don't know why she picked me out, but she said, "Did you know Elmer Smith died?" Well, we beat our way to Centralia for the funeral. Out of the clear sky there must have been five hundred lumberjacks and construction workers and Wobblies and friends of Wobblies. I guess that was about 1928. There weren't many lawyers like Elmer Smith. He fought so often he was disbarred as an attorney in the state and could only practice federal cases, but he gave decent attorney's advice on compensation cases. Finding an attorney to defend workers was a hard thing to do in those days.

The background to Centralia was our campaign to organize the lumber camps. We were carrying on a struggle to get the eight hour day. We wanted to get beds and decent living conditions. In the lumber camps, the beds were three bunks high and there were no baths. Workers were lousy and food was lousy. We ate pig jowls, pig tails, and pig feet. We'd say, "Pass the running gears," or "Pass the gate feeder." Breakfast would be oatmeal and bread with the worst coffee in the world. Everything was the cheapest you could get. Each man carried a couple of blankets in an empty sack to be used as a mattress. He'd have to go to the corral where the horses were kept and get straw to fill it. It smelled bad, especially in the middle of the tent, because most of them were tents, not real bunkhouses. There would be all those wet clothes, because nine months of the year Washington is full of water, so workers had to boil up and hang their clothes as close to the stove as they possibly could to dry them out. One way we harassed the company was to stop working after eight hours, or work two ten hour days and one four hour day and say that equals three eight hour days,

• *Washington timberbeasts in bunkhouse.*

and we'd pull out. We burned blankets whenever we could. Lots
of them wouldn't burn, so we threw gasoline on them and set them
on fire. It was a stinking mess. Some of the men hated to see their
blankets burn because they needed them to sleep in a boxcar, but
some of them liked it a lot. Whether you liked it or not, your
blankets were taken and thrown into the pile. It was the best way
to get some action. We got the blanket reforms. We got spring beds,
white sheets, two or four to a room instead of forty. We even got
better food. We ran the belly robber, the cook, out of camp unless
we got decent food. After a while we started to get pork chops
and rib steaks instead of joints, tails, livers, kidneys, and hearts.
A lot of these reforms didn't come until the early 1920s.

The IWW would strike from May Day on, and in the fall we'd
have a big strike, pulling all the camps we possibly could, traveling
over as many areas as possible. On May Day of 1923 we had the
workers pile their blankets into the square at Tacoma and burned
them. We did some sabotage too. One place in Washington we
moved a steam shovel across the railroad tracks when the Oriental
Limited was due. We were moving sections of rail as far ahead
as we possibly could. they had to stop the train and go hunt up
new rails and move that steam shovel off the tracks. That didn't

hurt anybody, but we did stop the train.

We used every tactic. When Woodrow Wilson took a trip to Seattle, we made up our minds to occupy as many blocks as we could. The men wore blue shirts and black jeans, and the women wore simple dresses. The idea was that all along the route they would be applauding Wilson, but when he came to that stretch anyone who started to applaud would be silenced real quick. We stood with folded arms as he passed up from Kings Street Station up Pike Street to the hotel. For the first block, he couldn't imagine what was going on, all those silent people. Then his body guard told him it was Wobblies. For the next three blocks, it was the same people with their arms folded just treating him as if he was some object to be pitied.

People always ask where the word *Wobbly* came from. According to legend it came from a strike in Vancouver. There was a Chinaman who fed the strikers but couldn't pronounce "W" properly. When he said "IWW" it sounded like "I Wobble Wobble" and from that came "Wobbly." Another version I heard was that *Wobbly* came from the wobble saw used by lumberjacks. No one really knows.

People forget how much the IWW believed in and preached education. For a time I went to Duluth, Minnesota, to the Working People's College, which the Finns were financing. They had good professors that were barred from many schools and were donating their services. We always had lots of songs and poems to liven things up. The only thing that used to bother me was that there weren't any decent toasts in the beer gardens. All they could say was *skoal* or *muchdo*. So I composed this one:

> To the sailors on the ocean, to the mucker in the mine,
> To the child slave in the factory, to the logger
>   in the pine;
> To the lonely social outcast, to the woman of the street,
> To those who've felt oppression, to the striker in defeat;
> To every son of labor, to every child of toil,
> This toast is dedicated in the hope that we may see
> A sturdy race of free men in an age that is to be.

I was born on November 7, 1905, the same day and the same year the IWW filed its papers of incorporation. When I joined up in 1919, I didn't know if there was going to be a revolution; but I knew there was going to be better conditions. That was what we were after, more for the immediate than for the ultimate. The ultimate was more or less what the philosophic anarchists and

BEWARE

GOOD PAY or BUM WORK

I.W.W.

ONE BIG UNION

WE NEVER FORGET

SABOTAGE

FOR INFORMATION ADDRESS I W W 66 W MADISON ST CHICAGO ILL U S A

socialists in there were talking about, pie in the sky, but I wanted the pork chops on the table right now. I wanted the ultimate too, but I didn't think we were going to get it because of the violence against us. You've got to fight violence with violence. You use the same tactics they use on you. You won't be able to use the ballot box, which is only a rattle box for children to play with. You have to reach out to get everyone the system doesn't want.

We were the first ones to give equality to women in industry: equal pay, equal hours, equal conditions. We advocated that way back in 1910, and we put it into effect whenever we got any power.

We also spent lots of time trying to organize Negroes. Ben Fletcher, one of our better organizers, went to the South for that. It was worth an organizer's life if he got caught. We offered free dues and free initiation to Negroes to come into the IWW, because they had so little. We did the same with the Chinese and Japanese. I organized a group of Hindus in Marysville, California. We had one bunch that wouldn't cooperate. They used a rag dipped in water instead of toilet paper, so I took turpentine and poured it into their water. When they went to use the rag for toilet paper, they had an unpleasant experience.

We never let up on what we wanted. We knew that until we got the economic power or the physical power to take it away from the employers, we could only get reforms. We used to sing songs like the "Internationale" and "The Red Flag." We used poems, toasts, leaflets, doggerel, speeches. I loved what Eugene V. Debs would say. He wrote beautiful pieces. He would talk about a world without prostitution, a world where the worker receives his full share, where the old people would receive a decent pension, a world that was not sped up, a world without wars, a world without crime and diseases.

The IWW did a lot for the working class, but we had weaknesses, too. One was that the IWW wouldn't sign an agreement with the employer, so we couldn't hold the conditions that we won. Second, we made the initiation and dues too cheap. The IWW fell into the hands of the migratory workers. They were less stable. The big split happened in 1924. Many of us wanted to see the two factions stay together, but it didn't work out.

Our success was being able to organize. The biggest thing a union can do is organize. No matter what the industry, a union can improve hours, wages, conditions, health, welfare. To get that, you have to have people walk thousands and thousands of miles on the picket lines. We did that. A lot of the benefits that exist came from our work. We helped the AFL, the UMW, all of them. The CIO used a lot of ex-Wobblies just like they used Communists to get themselves organized. They used sabotage, too. John L. Lewis' brother was organizing the building trades and would throw mustard seed into a sand pile, and two weeks later out of the wall would grow the finest crop of mustard you ever saw and no one could remove it. They borrowed that method from the IWW. I once got a watch from John L. Lewis for work I did.

I worked as a sailor on ships. I worked in construction. I worked in the woods. I worked in the harvest fields. I worked in restaurants. After I left the IWW in 1932, I became an organizer for other unions. I organized in San Francisco. Cement plants, water works, park employees, the Golden Gate workers—I organized all of them. In the IWW I learned that the working class and the employing class have nothing in common. Between those two classes, the struggle must go on until the working class organizes as a class and abolishes the wage system. Wesley Everest was taken out and castrated and hung up to a railroad bridge and then they buried his body no one knows where. Joe Hill was killed organizing against the Mormon Church in Utah construction. Frank Little was killed in Butte, Montana, for organizing the Anaconda copper mines. Many other Wobblies were killed, but nobody knows their names or who they were. They just waded in and shot them and took them and hung them and threw their bodies somewhere. If you didn't have any relatives or didn't keep any addresses, no one knows. That was why I came to believe in any kind of methods and means to overthrow the capitalist system. What more can you add?

As we come marching, marching, we
battle too for men,
For they are women's children, and
we mother them again.
Our lives shall not be sweated from
birth until life closes;
Hearts starve as well as bodies, give
us bread, but give us roses!
                    —James Oppenheim
                    "Bread and Roses"

WOMEN
IN TEXTILES

The IWW had committed itself to equality for female workers
from its very inception. Although only about a dozen delegates
to the founding convention were women, a reflection of the
attitudes in the established unions sending representatives, women
were given considerable visibility. On the podium at the opening
were Mother Jones, indefatigible advocate of miners' rights and
foe of child labor, and Lucy Parsons, an anarchist orator and
widow of one of the Haymarket martyrs.[1] Luella Twining, later
entrusted with managing Haywood's 1908 national tour, was a
voting delegate and chairperson of the ratification session. Shortly
after its founding, the IWW would draw brilliant female organizers
to its standard, the most notable being Elizabeth Gurley Flynn and
Matilda Rabinowitz. Such female IWWs spoke to, organized and
led male workers as well as females. While the IWW became
increasingly active in male-dominated industries after 1913, it
never abandoned efforts to organize women. The IWW was the
first American labor union to discuss the status of housework as

• *New England mill workers.*

a category of labor and the first to organize chambermaids and prostitutes.[2]

The major industry in the East earmarked for organization by the IWW was textile manufacturing. Approximately half of the textile workers were female, a large percentage under the age of twenty with many less than fourteen. Women played such a pivotal role in textiles that industrial unions without their full participation were inconceivable, just as industrial unions in Southern lumber had been inconceivable without the full participation of blacks. The IWW also understood that no textile strike would succeed if women who worked at home succumbed to the anti-union pressures generated by the employers and their allies in the press, public office, the school system, and the clergy. Women who did not themselves work in the mills had to be convinced that whatever the immediate hardships of a strike, there would be real long-term benefits for their families and community.

The conditions faced by textile workers were grim. Wages for all but a few skilled workers were so low that most were in chronic debt, and work conditions, especially for women and children, were lethal. At a time when the national life expectancy was nearly fifty years, over a third of all mill workers died before the age of twenty-six. Substandard housing was the rule in mill towns, which were usually organized into de facto language ghettos with the most recent immigrants having the worst accommodations.

When IWW organizers began to arrive at textile mills to proclaim the doctrine of industrial democracy, a substantial number of workers were interested. By 1908, after leading a number of minor strikes, the IWW could claim 5,000 members for its National Industrial Union of Textile Workers headed by James P. Thompson. The biggest textile challenge came four years later when pay cuts led to a groundswell of strike sentiment in Lawrence, Massachusetts. IWW Local 20 had been on the scene for more than four years, and its members had an excellent grasp of the conditions of the 60,000 Lawrence residents dependent on the mills for their livelihood. Prompted by local IWWs, the strikers sent for seasoned organizer Joe Ettor, an IWW orator who had already been in Lawrence, and Arturo Giovannitti, Secretary of the Italian Socialist Federation and editor of its organ, Il Proletario.

Faced with having to organize workers from twenty-four major national groups speaking twenty-two different languages, the Lawrence leadership devised an organizational structure that became the standard IWW mode of operation. Each language group was given representatives on the strike committee, which numbered from 250 to 300 members. All decisions regarding tactics and settlements were democratically voted on by the committee, with the IWW organizers acting strictly as advisors.

The Lawrence strikers realized that their battle went beyond wages and work conditions to address the question of the quality and purpose of life. Female strikers expressed their needs in an unforgettable phrase when they appeared on the picket line with a homemade placard declaring, "We Want Bread and Roses Too," a demand which became a fixture in the labor and feminist movements. But neither roses nor bread were possible without the most militant kind of strike and innovative worker tactics. Women would show the way on both scores. More female pickets than males were to be arrested for intimidating strikebreakers, and rank and file women provided decisive leadership at key moments in the strike.

Prohibited from massing before individual mills by law, the male and female strikers formed a moving picket line around the entire mill district! This human chain involving thousands of spirited workers moved twenty-four hours a day for the entire duration of the ten-week strike. Augmenting the awesome picket lines were frequent parades through town of from 3,000 to 6,000 strikers marching to militant labor songs. When a city ordinance was passed forbidding parades and mass meetings, the strikers

• Lawrence Daily Eagle, *February 19, 1912.*

improvised sidewalk parades in which twenty to fifty individuals locked arms and swept through the streets. They passed through department stores disrupting normal business and otherwise succeeded in bringing commerce to a halt. At night strikers serenaded the homes of scabs trying to get a good night's sleep, and in some cases the names of scabs were sent back to their native lands to shame their entire clan.

When striker Annie Lo Pezzo was killed during one of the demonstrations, Ettor and Giovannitti were arrested on murder charges; they were said to have provoked workers to illegal acts which in turn resulted in the death. Their places were promptly taken by Bill Haywood, Elizabeth Gurley Flynn, William Trautman, and Carlo Tresca. Haywood's arrival in Lawrence was tumultuous. Fifteen thousand strikers greeted him at the railroad station and 25,000 listened to him speak on the Lawrence Commons. During the course of the strike, there were dynamite schemes by employers, a proclamation of martial law, the death of a Syrian teenage boy from a militiaman's bayonet, and repeated physical confrontations between strikers and law enforcement groups. Women again played a critical role when it was decided to have the children of the strikers cared for by sympathizers in other cities. After some groups of children had left Lawrence, the army resolved to block further removals. In the ensuing physical confrontation, many women were beaten and two pregnant women miscarried. The brutal incident led to the national publicity and governmental hearings that resulted in victory for the strikers.

In the wake of the Lawrence triumph came strikes in other textile centers under IWW leadership and a successful campaign to free Ettor and Giovannitti. Prominent women such as socialist humanitarian Helen Keller, birth control activist Margaret Sanger and AFL organizer Mary Kenney O'Sullivan enthusiastically supported various IWW initiatives. Textile owners not yet faced with strikes began to grant wage increases unilaterally in hopes of averting unionization. The *Detroit News* estimated that 438,000 textile workers received nearly fifteen million dollars in raises as an indirect consequence of the Lawrence strike, with the biggest gains scored by the 275,000 workers in New England.

For a brief season, the IWW was on the threshold of unionizing textiles and redrawing the labor map of America. But the IWW victory never materialized. Among the IWW's problems was that the organization had not yet mastered the techniques of maintaining large locals on a permanent basis, once the pressure of a strike was over. A year after the strike in Lawrence, local membership had fallen from ten thousand to under one thousand, as the union failed to counter new employer pressures. Of more immediate consequence was the eight-month strike which took place in Paterson, New Jersey.

Paterson, the center of the nation's silk industry, employed 25,000 workers in dying and manufacturing. Late in 1912, the mill owners embarked on a policy of speedups and wage cuts. The result was a spontaneous strike and a call for IWW assistance. The tactics recently used elsewhere with such great success were again employed, and top IWW organizers led by William Haywood and Elizabeth Gurley Flynn were constantly on the scene. Nonetheless the strike did not go well. One factor was an unprecedented rate of arrests, which created a chronic shortage of funds for strike benefits, legal fees, fines and bail.

In May of 1913, John Reed, just beginning to achieve fame as a socialist journalist, proposed to solve the financial logjam and bring a national spotlight to the strike with a pageant to be staged in New York City's Madison Square Garden.[3] The pageant was announced in red lights ten feet high spelling out "IWW" on the side of Madison Square Garden. Although a propagandistic knockout with fifteen thousand people in attendance, the pageant was a financial fizzle, barely covering its costs. The event also created petty jealousies among strikers over who would take part. The pageant seems to have drained energy and funds that might have been more usefully employed in Paterson itself, but the show established a precedent for fundraising and publicity that would be followed by other radical groups, especially by the Communist Party in the 1930s and 1940s.

The Paterson strikers operated under disadvantages that had not existed in other textile centers. The mill operators saw themselves as the last line of defense for the industry and were prepared to stand firm whatever the economic costs. Unlike Lawrence, where the American Woolen Company dominated the city, there was no one mill in Paterson that could be singled out as the major target. The Paterson silk manufacturers also had other plants in Pennsylvania, where the workers did not strike. Their production guaranteed income to the owners however long the Paterson strike might last. A self-inflicted weakness was that the strike committee often disregarded the advice of the IWW, particularly on issues of solidarity. Sensing this weakness, the owners eventually offered plant by plant settlements, a practice which pit some of the skilled against the unskilled, and some of the native born against the foreign born.

The Paterson strike was officially terminated in August and

marked the end of IWW momentum in textiles. Individual units in various locations remained active for years afterward, but the organization was never able to mount another offensive such as that of 1905 to 1913. The fragile alliance that had been developing with some feminists withered, and decades would pass before the needs of working women resurfaced as major items on labor's agenda.

A defeat sometimes demonstrates an organization's characteristics even more vividly than victory. Such is the case with Paterson, where the IWW managed to implant visionary ideals in the midst of a brutal losing bid for immediate gains. Sophie Cohen and Irma Lombardi were among the Paterson workers who hurled themselves into self-generated, point-of-production activism. Cohen, who later became a nurse, retained her IWW membership, and her views reflect the thinking of rank and file Wobbly women. Lombardi, who continued to be a textile worker for forty years, is more representatives of the tens of thousands of women in the Northeast who responded to the talks of the Gurley Flynns. Although an enthusiastic striker, once the battle was over Lombardi lost contact with the IWW. One can posit that there must have been many like her who had once embraced the IWW and would have done so again if presented the opportunity.

• *Matilda Rabinowitz and fellow workers.*

Sophie Cohen

Paterson had a prison-like feeling when you walked through the narrow streets where the mills were. They were red brick buildings with small, dirty windows set very high. The mills were next to the Passaic River. We lived about two blocks from the river, so when I had to bring lunch to my father, I had to go uphill. Whenever you walked from the center of town, you walked up.

My father collapsed at one of the mills when I was young, and he was told never to go back again. That was a terrible time for us. My mother had a child that died during birth and my little brother died from diptheria. Somehow, though, my mother and father got together with another family, and they managed to put a deposit on a farm outside of town. I remember the fields and how hard they worked, but they couldn't keep up the payments. That's when we came back to Paterson.

My father couldn't go back to the mills, but he was able to set up a laundry. We'd get shirts and things from our family doctor and other people who were a bit wealthier and could afford to send lace curtains and things like that to a laundry. Childhood was not unhappy for us. For Christmas or Hanukkah, my father would take us to Broadway where there was an Italian fruit shop and he'd buy big California oranges. That was a big treat. There was one group that said it would give toys to all the children of the workers. I think it was the Salvation Army, but I'm not sure. My sister and I went. We stood in line and went into a house where they gave us a little package. They said not to open it up until we got home. But we couldn't wait. We opened it up and found a broken toy. That was the closest to toys we ever got. We used to play with mud pies. We dug holes and things like that. Sometimes, my father would take us to the woods. One thing that was very different from now is when we had a meeting, everyone went. Adults and children attended as long as they were part of the shop. We didn't divide ourselves by age.

There were a lot of nationalities in Paterson. A lot of the textile workers were Italian, and there were Jewish people, Poles, and some Germans. When we went to a picnic or mass meeting, we didn't care if someone was a different nationality. The children played together and the people talked together, as well as they could. The children would be sent over to get beer for the adults. It made no difference whether you were Italian or Jewish or Polish. The barrels of beer were for everyone. There was a lot of singing too, at the picnics and at the meetings.

During the strike, Carlo Tresca was one of our leaders. You didn't have to understand Italian to feel what he was saying. Everyone spoke with accents but that didn't get in the way. There was a refrain everyone knew:

> *Do you like Mr. Boss? No, no, no!*
> *Do you like Miss Flynn? Yes, yes, yes!*
> *The IWW! Hurray! Hurray!*

A lot of speakers would use that in their talks. They'd yell out, "Do you like Mr. Boss?" and people would laugh and shout back as loud as they could, "No, no, no!" Those were tremendous events for us when we were children.

We children didn't have many entertainments. Only three stand out in my mind. One was the Italian organ grinder. He had a little monkey who tried to get money into his cup. There was little money, but after a lot of giggling, screaming, and singing, he would sometimes get a penny. The minute he would get a coin, the organ grinder would leave. That was all he was waiting for, but in the meantime, we had a lot of fun with him and his monkey. On Fridays a violinist came. He would play and tell the story of the fire that happened in the Triangle Shirt Waist Company in New York. He would try to get some pennies too, but he wanted to make us aware of political issues. The other thing we did was walk to the Passaic Falls. Other than that, there was school and the mills.

When I was graduating from the eighth grade, the principal came around to tell us that there was a new shirt company opening that was perfect for young people because it was not noisy and dirty like the textile mills. The factory was offering five dollars a week, which seemed a tremendous amount then. I was only fourteen at the time, and girls my age were not allowed to come to work at the usual starting time of seven. We waited until eight and then stayed until five; on Saturdays, we worked until one. At the end of the week, we got either $3.75 or $3.95, because they had deducted the hour we didn't come in. Our job was to box shirts. The conditions were dreadful. If you went to the bathroom more than twice a day and were more than a few minutes, you were reported to the office by the floorwalker.

Most of the girls were taught how to weave by their parents. Since my father was not in the mills at that time, I went to an office where the bolts of cloth were shipped. In return for helping them, I was taught how to weave. They never paid me, and as soon as I thought I knew enough, I left. Soon afterwards, I went with one of the girls I had met at a Wobbly picnic to look for a job. I told them I was a weaver. It was all right for a while, then a filling got stuck. I didn't know what to do. I got so frightened I never went back after lunch. I didn't even go to ask for the money I had already earned.

• *Interior of Paterson mill, 1910s.*

I finally did learn to weave and got my first job as a weaver. One of the big issues for us was the loom system. They used to get people to work four and even six looms at a time. That's the reason men brought their wives with them. It was too much for one person. If a thread broke or a piece fell down, the fine threads would be flawed. You couldn't let this happen, so you had to stop the loom to fix it. When you did that, you weren't making cloth. You had to keep going from the front. You had to inject the filling and then go around the back to see how the threads there were. To keep four or six looms going was just impossible. Even if you somehow managed, you still didn't earn enough for the fundamentals of living.

I remember the clanging of those looms, the sound of steel against steel. You couldn't speak with one another unless you shouted. Many of the weavers brought a piece of wood to stand on to get relief from the cement floor. It didn't relieve anything for me. The first time I walked out of the mill, I couldn't hear normally and although I knew my feet were touching the ground, it felt strange. After a time, I got used to the noise. There seemed to be a certain rhythm to the loom. It encouraged me to sing. The only way I could endure that work was to sing along to the rhythm of the loom. Most of the discomfort could be forgotten that way. Maybe that's why we used to sing so many Wobbly songs.

About this time, the AFL tried to organize the school teachers. A number of the teachers were quite sympathetic. They felt sorry for young girls who could only go to the eighth grade and then were sent to the mills. They started to teach us in small groups on Sunday. We'd read Shakespeare and Dreiser, and they tried to help as much as they could. When the school system found out, the teachers were fired. There was never a union for them.

Everyone worked long days then. My mother would go to the farmers' market at four in the morning pushing a baby carriage. The farmers had come from the night before, and anything they didn't sell, they would let you have cheap or for nothing. Sometimes she'd get potatoes or big sacks of vegetables. The neighbors would come in and they'd divide up whatever they got. Before I started working in the mills, my mother used to send me to the butcher to buy meat. If you bought meat, he'd always give you a lot of bones, and some days you would get liver. I would ask for liver "for my cat." Of course, it wasn't for the cat. My mother always had a big pot of soup on the stove. People would often come to ask my father to help him find a job or to discuss a problem. My mother always managed to have a bowl of soup to offer. It was always from the bones, but to get the bones and liver free, you had to buy some meat.

My parents could read, write, and speak German, Russian, and Hebrew. Our home became a nucleus for people who wanted to write home but were illiterate. They would come to our house to have my mother write their letters. But people from Warsaw and Lodz tended to be well-educated; and they were the ones who became leaders in our strike. People used to meet in our house to talk about conditions. You weren't allowed to belong to a union or organize one. If you were heard talking about that at work, you would be blacklisted immediately. Many of the Polish people worked in the dye factories. The smell was so bad that when we'd pass by, we had to hold our breath and run. Even from the outside, we could hardly breathe. They worked in water up to their knees. The clothes most of us wore were hand-me-downs. People would crowd in about three rooms and then take a boarder to make ends meet. You couldn't get credit from the butcher, but the grocer used to sell a few odd pieces of meat which helped. Many of the men couldn't take it. Instead of going home with their pay, many headed straight for the saloon. There was one on our corner, and I would see children running to find their fathers, or wives coming to see if they could rescue some money before the husbands drank it all. I couldn't blame the men that much. There was nothing to look forward to after pay day. They had to start the same thing all over again. Conditions became worse and worse until either you had to just stop living or become a rebel. That's when the IWW came in.

Everyone would go out to the IWW picnics and meetings. Haywood came to speak. Gurley Flynn came. There was Tresca, Scott Nearing, Norman Thomas, Roger Baldwin. I remember once I didn't want to go. I said, "Pop, all they do is talk." He said, "Listen." One time they refused to let the IWW meet in the Turn Hall. We had to walk all the way to Haledon, a small town outside Paterson where they had a socialist mayor who allowed us to have picnics in the woods and to hold meetings.

Gurley Flynn looked just like the pictures we see of her now. She was young, vibrant, enthusiastic. She wasn't really a good speaker, but she gave so much of herself in her talks. She would come at night to the soup kitchens. There were big caldrons of soup set up in a lot next to the church and she would get up on a platform. There were red flares around her, and she'd get them singing and then she'd talk with them. It was just the thing people needed to keep them together and give them courage.

Although my father was very sympathetic to the IWW, he couldn't be a member; he had a store. But he always went to the

• *Children of Paterson strikers in New York City, 1913.*

meetings and picnics. When he spoke of Scott Nearing, he would lower his voice as if he was talking about a person so great he was almost holy. We liked Haywood, too. He seemed a tower of strength. He was a big fellow and had one eye closed. He didn't wear a patch. The eye was just closed.

It's important to realize that we were very proud to be Americans. Even though we were radical, strikers always carried the flag. In those days, during the elections, newspapers would flash images on sheets attached to the side of the buildings. Candidates would soapbox in front of them and sometimes they'd have arguments. My father always took me, and he would say, "This is America. They say whatever they want during the election; but afterwards, they shake hands. It isn't like other countries where they shoot one another and kill one another. This is America."

During the actual strike, most of the children were sent away to people in New York. They wore red sashes and were put into trucks, yelling and screaming like it was a lot of fun. They were in front of our laundry and I wanted to go too, but my father said, "Shhh, you have something to eat. They have nothing." It wasn't easy for the families to give up their children, but my father was right. There was no income and the strike fund was low. The grocer fed most of the workers on credit, and there were soup kitchens. The strike lasted until the summer, then groups began to fall away.

The police would be violent when there was picketing, but the Paterson workers were never violent. That was the last thing on our minds. We had no guns. I don't believe anyone I knew could operate a gun. There was one Italian man shot on the picket line. There was a collection to raise money for his widow, who, I think, opened an Italian grocery afterwards. The police also raided homes. There was a Wobbly who had important files in his room. One night after an IWW dance, someone suggested we go to New York. I had never been to New York, to Greenwich Village, and a whole group of us decided to do it. We went to Long John Silver's, the Pirates' Den, where the waiters wore patches for atmosphere. We missed the last train home and didn't get back until dawn, on the milk run. There was someone waiting to tell us that the Wobbly's room had been raided. I saw it. The room was in a private house, but they had pulled open all the drawers and taken things away. The police weren't gentle, and of course they arrested many people.

We had a big pageant for the strike. That was much more our way of doing things. John Reed was involved in that. It was to show exactly what had happened in Paterson. It showed how the looms had stopped, how a striker was shot, how the picket lines were. Although the pageant seemed to siphon off some of the energy we had, there really wasn't much more that could have been done. The employers were stronger. The workers had nothing but their enthusiasm and courage.

I wasn't an official organizer, but when I became a weaver, a girlfriend and I would take jobs in unorganized factories and try to organize them. We would refuse the four looms, saying it was too much for us. Because we were young girls, we were permitted to work only two. After a few weeks, we would hand out leaflets and call for an organizing meeting. We looked so innocent that the managers never thought we were capable of even believing in a union. In one place, they locked us out. They called the police, and we had to get our pay at a little booth. When the police handed us the pay and our tools, I refused the tools because I considered the factory to be on strike. The cop got angry and said if I didn't take them there, I could come for them at the station. Rather than be organized, that particular factory closed and left town to start again somewhere in Pennsylvania.

The companies never stopped putting the pressure on. If you said you were an IWW, it was like saying you were a criminal. For years there were people who would not let you know they had been IWWs. They would deny it out of simple fear. If you were an IWW in Paterson, you were blacklisted. I got a lesson on how much they feared the IWW when I was just starting to work. I used to teach children on the block some IWW songs. I'd always come home for lunch, and one day while I was eating, there was a bang on the door. My mother, who was very short, opened the door, and there was a gigantic policemen standing there. He said he wanted to see me. She led him to the table where I was eating. He looked down at me, and he must have realized how ridiculous the situation was. He had been sent to find a dangerous rebel, and there was a fifteen year old girl eating lunch. He left. But imagine! A little girl sang a song in school and the teacher reported it and the principal called the police and the police came to my door. For a song.

I guess I had no choice about becoming a rebel. The first dress I ever bought that was mine was after I had earned my first pay as a weaver. I wanted to go to a Wobbly dance, but I had to bring that money home, because we never had any extra spending money. On the way home, I saw a pretty dress. I opened my paycheck and took some money out and bought the dress. When I got home I told my mother someone saw me looking at the dress, bought it, and gave it to me. It was a ridiculous story. It was having to make excuses like that that kept you fighting.

The IWW left people with a taste for organization. Every time workers win a strike, it helps straighten out their backs a little bit more and lifts their heads a bit higher. Even though the big strike was lost in Paterson, there was a feeling of togetherness among the workers. We had a medium of expression. From then on, there were a series of strikes and every shop had to be reorganized. Every shop refought the eight hour day all the way down the line—and the four loom system. We used to carry placards: "Eight hours work—eight hours play—eight hours sleep." Well, there was always some shop going on strike for one reason or another. The thing in 1913 that we really acted on and won was the two loom system.

I'm still with the IWW. The AFL-CIO was organized along the lines of a big corporation with the president receiving a fabulous amount and the workers just like commodities. The IWW was more than a union. It wanted to bring forth a new form of society. The IWW taught that the worker has nothing in common with the employer. The average worker still doesn't understand that. The eight hour day and pensions are taken for granted. They can't understand there was a time when the word *vacation* was foreign. The IWW tried to educate people to be more than horses, more than cogs in a wheel. The IWW never had high paid officials. How can a president who earns so much understand the plight of a working mother who has to deposit her child in a day care center and run off to her job still worrying about a fever the child might have? The president worries about the best college to send his kids to. They can't understand each other. There is a big division. The leaders have political jobs. They need the workers so they can exist, but they do not function in the interest of the worker, of the working class.

The IWW fought for new values, for a society where every person can be a full human being. We saw that men were bored from doing the same ritual work, day after day, week after week. Of course, they drank too much. We had a slogan: "You can't fight booze and the boss at the same time." We were against drink and in favor of education. What the worker needs most is not more pennies per hour but education. We thought that when workers got to understand their situation, they could have a general strike and through the general work stoppage, workers would get their various goals.

If you are not a rebel, it is easy to be pessimistic. How can people live with themselves? I fought whenever I could. During the Sacco and Vanzetti struggle, I soapboxed on South Street. I told the audience that we should cut the powerlines so they couldn't electrocute them. Another time, I was there and got swept into the safety of a restaurant when the police came through swinging clubs from their horses. When I moved to New York, it was different than Paterson. There were no mills. But I would work for and organize dances for the General Recruiting Union. I never charged any expenses. When my husband was working—he was a carpenter—I thought, how can you take money for doing things for the organization? We couldn't. We struggled as best we could and we always sang those wonderful songs.

Irma Lombardi

When the big strike came in Paterson, I was seventeen. I had been working three years by then. I was all for it. We thought we were going to change the world. When you're young, you do have dreams. I was always on the picket lines, every single day. We'd just walk peacefully, sing, and even have fun until the cops came. They would start chasing us, swing with their clubs from horseback. Many of us were hurt badly and many were arrested. There weren't just young people out there. There were middle-aged people and some really old people—people in their eighties—who were still working. There were lots of Italians and Poles, Jewish, Germans—a little bit of everything.

We kept it up for eight months. We walked around so much my father used to buy a piece of leather to sole our shoes. He had a garden and we ate all fresh vegetables. We also ate a lot of soup and oatmeal. There was one Italian shoemaker who would fix shoes for nothing during the strike. A lot of people went to him. The baker, the butcher, the milkman—they all delivered our stuff even though no one could pay. When the strike was over and we started working again, my father began to pay them back. Eventually he paid all his debts. One man told him, "If everybody had done like you, Marcelli, it would be all right." But a lot didn't pay.

During the strike a lot of forces were put against us. The morning newspaper was one. That newspaper criticized the strikers and the organizers, especially the organizers. "Agitators. A bunch of agitators are in Paterson," that's what they would write. I used to get mad reading it. I said they aren't agitating us, they are telling us the truth. Organizers don't break laws by helping poor people. The evening paper was against us too, but not like the other one. And the priests were no help. They would urge children to ask their fathers to go back to work. The teachers did the same. They would say, "Tell your father to go back to work." Now they had no business doing that. Today, teachers and police have their own unions.

Gurley Flynn called a meeting just for the women one day. She started with that lovely way of hers. She looked at us and said,

"Would you like to have nice clothes?" We replied, "Oh, yes." "Would you like to have nice shoes?" "Oh, yes," we shouted. "Well, you can't have them. Your bosses' daughters have those things!" We got mad. We knew it was true. We had shoes with holes, and they had lovely things. Then she said, "Would you like to have soft hands like your bosses' daughters?" And we got mad all over again. She was a beautiful speaker. She got to be an idol with us. We adored all our leaders. Haywood had a terrific voice that could fill a whole hall, even if you were in the balcony. Tresca talked in Italian. Then there was Lessing. I believe he was German. Gurley and Pat Quinlan spoke in English.

We didn't have trouble persuading people to strike. They were happy to fight back. They were disgusted with those conditions. By the time you got home, you were dead tired and there still wasn't enough money. On Saturday when I finished at twelve, I would go downtown to work from one to nine at night to get another seventy-five cents. Then I could buy some underwear and other things I needed. That was the way it was.

During the picketing, if the cops saw a few of us on a sidewalk, they'd come and chase us as though we were nothing. I would say, "What do you think we are?" "Oh, that's all right, keep going, keep going," they'd say. "What do you mean, 'Keep going'? I'm not doing anything wrong. You're the one who's doing wrong." I had a friend named Charlie who was a cop. One day I told him, "I'm surprised at you. All right, it's your job; but if a thing isn't right, you should refuse to do it. You were a weaver once, before you were a cop. Don't you remember? I remember. So tell your Chief Bimson to go some place." He was no good, that Bimson.

One day we were in front of Wideman's and there were a lot of strikebreakers who had been imported from the West Indies. We started yelling. Then there was some shooting. I don't think it was our cops. I think it was the militia. One man was on his porch, holding his baby, and he was killed. Then they were clubbing everyone. I said to that cop, "What are you people doing?" He said he was following Chief Bimson's orders. We never expected things like that: to be clubbed, to be shot at, to be killed. Never.

I don't remember the strikers doing anything violent. It was mostly the police. Oh, I remember one incident. When scabs would go to work, we would go to the shop and holler at them. One day, we heard a loom running and a man got so excited he threw a rock. We all ran. He threw that one rock and bango, we ran for the trolley cars. It did make you mad, because you knew that if we went back with more money, the scabs would benefit too. There was one woman who would strike but not picket. She said, "I'll stay home and do housework." I said, "Will you? When we get our raise, you'll get yours too, won't you?" She said, "Yes, that's true." I said, "Well, you better picket." From then on, she did.

Another time me and a little Jewish lady who had been in the revolution in Russia got arrested. We were picketing, both little short women, we were picketing and these two cops were watching. Imagine how I felt when one put a hand on my shoulder and the other on hers. They said, "Come on," and we went. They had a little jail right next to the police station. The judge was sitting up there with us in front with a cop on each side. One cop said, "You know what she called me—a g.d. snake." I looked at the judge and said, "Your honor, I never use that kind of language." He looks down at me and says, "Case dismissed," and looks at the cop, "See you understand right from now on." The week after, the other cop tried to date me out. I said, "I'm sorry, I don't go out with cops."

And he was nice too.

After we lost the strike, we had lots of trouble. Five of us Italians went to work in a mill but got fired right away. We didn't know there was someone talking to the boss. Then when we went for jobs, they must have had our names because no one would take us. Finally, I went to a German factory, Biers. They were nice. The man said, "I know all about you," but he gave me a job anyway. I worked in the mills until I was fifty-one years old. Then I stayed home to take care of my father. I was a jacquard weaver. That's making dye goods: prints and patterns. You had to stand there watching your shuttle going back and forth, pulling your handle, letting her go, getting your smash, working up a backache getting it in.

The unions have changed. Bad people have infiltrated them. Those days an organizer would have patches on his pants. They weren't out for money. They were for the people, and they were good. The rebels didn't hurt anybody. They were for the rights of the people. I've been a rebel all my life. You just assert yourself and say how you feel. All the rebels I know are great people. I knew a rebel they used to call an anarchist. They made fun of him. But that man, when there was someone in need—and he needed himself because he was poor—he'd take up a collection. He'd get a quarter from this one and a nickel from another until he had a little something to help. Once a woman lost her husband, and this man went around collecting for the funeral. Do you call that bad?

The IWW stood for the Industrial Workers of the World. Work, good wages, and respect: that's what they wanted for the workers. To be people, not nobodies. They used to talk about owning the factories which I think would have been good. We would have all worked happily, gotten profits for ourselves instead of for one man or two. What was wrong about that? They were telling the truth. While the others are making millions, you're making nothing. That's what they talked about. If there were more people in the world like that, it would be better. Big Bill Haywood was a wonderful person, really a great person. We would say, "We're with you a hundred percent, Bill." That's how we felt, because we loved those people so much. We have such wonderful memories of the whole bunch.

I don't know what hapened to the IWW after the strike. I never heard anything anymore. That hurt me because I felt for certain they would take over and be our union. That's what I was looking for, but that didn't happen. The good people are always put out of business. I trusted them. Every word they said was true and sincere. They meant everything they said to us. If things had been fixed up with the IWW in those days, Paterson would have won. I think that's what deteriorated Paterson. That it didn't happen. Who's to blame? The employers and our government in Paterson for being against the workers.

Let me add a little bit of family history. My father was a loom fixer in Italy. They had a strike and the bosses called each man to ask who was the first to stop working. None of them would answer so they were all fired and put on a blacklist. Since there were only two factories in town, my father decided it was time to go to America. My mother was about to have a baby, so she had to stay behind. Later he sent money and we all came to America in steerage. At first, my father would work sixty hours a week, then it was cut to ten hours on weekdays and five on Saturdays. He was not afraid to strike. He was in one in 1901 when the militia came. Luckily, my father was short. Otherwise, he would have had a bullet through his head. Instead it went through his hat. That's the way things were in those days. But he was not disappointed in this country. He loved America. He really loved it. He said it wasn't America's fault; it was the mill owners'. He didn't blame his hard life on America.

SABOTAGE

Elizabeth Gurley Flynn

Ten Cents

I.W.W. Publishing Bureau
112 Hamilton Av.
CLEVELAND · OHIO

R. H. C.

> ...the help yelled for help. Bill Quint was
> sent out from IWW headquarters in Chicago
> to give them some action. He was against the
> strike, an open walkout. He advised the old
> sabotage racket, staying on the job and
> gumming things up from the inside. But that
> wasn't active enough for the Personville crew.
> They wanted to put themselves on the map,
> make labor history.
> —Dashiell Hammett
> Red Harvest

THE
HOME GUARD

A major goal of the newly formed IWW in 1905 was to organize
workers in light and heavy industries east of the Mississippi. This
work force was termed the "home guard," because, unlike
itinerants, industrial workers were eager to establish roots in a
specific geographic area and begin family life as soon as possible.
The Western miners who made up the bulk of the founding
membership of the IWW also tended to be geographically stable
and thought the Eastern home guard would make congenial allies.
Although ultimately unable to win the day for industrial unionism,
the IWW organizing campaigns would revitalize traditions
originating in the nineteenth century and create a militant legacy
the CIO would profit from twenty years later.

One of the historic IWW-led strikes of the era took place in 1906
when three thousand General Electric workers in Schenectady,
New York, carried out the first recorded sitdown strike in the
United States, setting a pattern for radical direct action among
electrical workers that would endure for generations. A year later

• Boone Tire Factory, Chippewa Falls, Wisconsin, 1913.

the IWW scored another significant victory when it led six hundred workers (mainly Hungarian immigrants) against the American Tube and Stamping Company of Bridgeport, Connecticut. Elsewhere in the Northeast, gains were made for shoemakers, transit workers, bakers and restaurant workers.

The IWW's public debut in the industrial Midwest came in 1909. At a subsidiary of U.S. Steel located at McKees Rocks, six miles south of Pittsburgh, IWW organizers guided the first successful steel strike in more than a decade. They mobilized five thousand workers of sixteen nationalities at a plant whose erratic payment policies and unsafe conditions were notorious in an industry where monopoly control denied labor any inherent rights. The savage contest took the lives of a trooper, two strikebreakers, and eight strike participants. Other successes against the steel trust came at two plants outside of Chicago. This trio of victories soon proved to be exceptions as management grew ever more ruthless in its anti-union stance, using spies, hoodlums, and dismissals to destroy all functioning IWW and AFL units. A hard fought but losing battle in New Castle, Pennsylvania, was a particularly harsh blow to IWW hopes. The reality was that the ill-financed and fragile IWW was no match for the financial and political clout of Big Steel. Isolated units survived for a time and there would be a massive national strike in 1919, but industrial unionism would not prevail in steel until the 1930s.

A byproduct of the short-term successes of the IWW in steel were regional locals of considerable strength. In the Chicago area, the IWW was able to organize hundreds of clothing and construction workers. In Pittsburgh, the IWW organized Jewish, black, and Irish stogie makers who had been neglected by the formerly powerful Knights of Labor. These cigar locals enjoyed strong support from ethnic communities and survived into the period of the First World War. They are noteworthy in another respect for they were able to maintain a union shop without the formality of a signed contract. In spite of such limited successes, the IWW organizers active in the Midwest, like those in New England, were learning that small isolated locals could not survive as more than holding actions or propaganda hubs unless an entire industry or locale could be organized in relative swift and decisive actions.

Prospects for such a campaign loomed in Akron, Ohio, in 1913. Heartened by the IWW victory in Lawrence, militant rubber workers asked the organization to furnish advisors. The IWW was soon leading strikes at Goodyear, Goodrich and Firestone. The majority of the fifteen thousand strikers were American-born and male, but at least a thousand were female and some fifteen hundred were immigrants, mainly from Hungary and Germany. The strike ran concurrent with the Paterson silk strike and Haywood tirelessly shuttled between the two cities, often under the threat of violence. As in the steel industry, the strategic position of the employers proved insurmountable. The workers were not financially able to endure a long strike and did not have the political or organizational might to stem the flow of strikebreakers. With a general economic downturn exacerbating the economic hardships, the historic uprising of the rubber workers ended in defeat.

A more favorable set of circumstances seemed to exist in Detroit, the emerging auto capital. In 1911, George Trautman had spent three months bringing together IWW sympathizers into Auto Workers Industrial Union Local 16. Two years later, Matilda Rabinowitz, famed for her organizing in textiles and fresh from working with the Pittsburgh stogie makers, arrived in motor city to direct an IWW offensive. The IWW plan called for short strikes with precisely defined goals. The culmination of IWW agitation along these lines was a week-long strike involving six thousand workers at Studebaker, the first major strike anywhere in the auto industry. The walkout only produced moderate gains, but the action was so troubling to the employers that prevention of further strikes of this kind was cited by Ford Motor Company officials a year later when they announced their precedent-smashing wage increases, which lifted the pay of auto workers to five dollars for an eight-hour day. The IWW local continued to function, but no other major attempt to organize took place until the 1930s when the Detroit IWW introduced autoworkers to the sitdown strike.[1]

After 1914, the IWW shifted its concentration to workers west of the Mississippi, where various locals were making spectacular gains. The units in heavy industries were left in place with the hope that a rejuvenated IWW would return to finish the task begun, a perspective undone by the repression of World War I. In spite of its immediate failures, the IWW left a formidable legacy in heavy industry. When the CIO unions developed in the 1930s, the factories and cities where the IWW had done its best organizing and achieved its greatest successes emerged as CIO bastions. This was partly due to the fact that these locations were ideal for industrial unionism, but the pronounced militancy of these sites must be attributed in some measure to the massive propaganda carried on by the IWW and the substantial number of workers who had been schooled in IWW methods.

Len De Caux, who was at the center of national CIO press

activities for twenty years, wrote of his fellow CIO militants, "When the CIO lefts let down their hair, it seemed that only the youngest had no background of Wobbly associations."[2] In a loving memoir of his years in the IWW, James Cannon, an activist in the Akron strike of 1913, described the IWW as "the great anticipation."[3] He depicted the IWW as a dress rehearsal for the CIO in the same manner that the failed 1905 uprising in Russia was a dress rehearsal for the revolutions of 1917. His view that "the CIO became possible only after and because the IWW had championed and popularized the notion of industrial unionism in word and deed" finds considerable documentation in studies of specific CIO unions. Very detailed research in the auto and steel unions, for example, demonstrates that scores of officials, mainly at the local level, had been significantly involved in the IWW.

Not least among the IWW achievements was the dismantling of the proposition that the foreign born could not be good trade unionists. Strikes had been lost, but the losses did not stem from workers' lack of solidarity or discipline. The corporations were just too strong economically and could command the support of all levels of government whenever needed. This imbalance of power would not change until employer power was crippled by the impact of the Great Depression and labor power was enhanced by the pro-union policies of Roosevelt's New Deal.

Interstate job hunts, the dynamics of ethnic communities, governmental repression, and the relationship of the IWW to conventional unions dominate the memories of Dominic Mignone, Irving Abrams, Henry Pfaff and Vaino Konga. The IWW outlook accents their accounts of the interaction between different radical, liberal, and ethnic forces of the era, an interaction indicating the IWW was not a unique social deviation but part of a profound mass questioning of what the nature of the American social order should be.

Dominic Mignone expands on previous descriptions of the Paterson strike by detailing some of the internal strife and support in the largest ethnic group involved. Irving Abrams relates how threadbare militant workers rushed from city to city trying to maintain the radical momentum set off by the victory in Lawrence. After finally settling in Chicago, Abrams would drift to full-fledged anarchism and for years would be Conservator of the Haymarket Memorial. Henry Pfaff is noteworthy in that he joined the IWW twice. His first enrollment, during the landmark Akron rubber strike of 1913, was like that of thousands of other foreign born workers in basic industry who took out red cards in a burst of militant rage without truly entering or understanding the IWW;

in Pfaff's case, six years after his membership, intervening work experiences and examination of political alternatives brought him back to the IWW for what became a lifetime commitment. Vaino Konga concludes with a focus on the Finnish communities which were energetic home guard bastions for the IWW in Minnesota, North Dakota, the upper penninsula of Michigan, and northern Wisconsin.

Dominic Mignone

When the strike in Paterson begun, I was working in a mill and I made up my mind to walk. There was another fellow with me, but the rest of them worked on. We reported to the IWW, but they said they couldn't do nothing about that particular mill right then. They did ask us to join them. I did, and I stayed with them for the duration of the strike. I don't want to call myself a revolutionary, but I was very active on the picket lines. I didn't want to miss anything, not even one hour.

The IWW instructed you to fight morally. I got to convince you not to go to work, not punch you in the nose. We would go from house to house to the scabs and urge them not to go to the mills. We would boycott them, too. For my part, if they are still living, I still boycott them. I don't want to recognize them, because they betrayed us. A lot of the societies would expel members who were scabs. Well, it was against the law to expel them, but they were made not welcome and they quit.

The IWW had a food store on the corner of Prospect and Allison for the men with families. Young fellows, like me, got a ticket to go and eat in a restaurant. We had a place called Thomas Dillon, a bar and restaurant. The card was for thirty-five cents a day, but that was more than enough. The bar used to have a shelf with slices of bread, sardines in oil, Swiss cheese, salami, cold cuts, and this and that. For five cents you got a big glass of beer. For dinner hour, they gave us a bowl of soup with crackers, then spaghetti and meat balls. That was all right. The money came from collections. Since I had a lot of friends in Newark, I went there with a friend and stayed two days collecting money. We went from one saloon to another, one center to another. When we finished Newark, we went to Elizabeth. We gave the money to the union. No humbug. Some people moved the money from one pocket to another like it was their money. But not us. Our collections went into the union fund. We even turned in the receipts.

The parish of St. Michael, the Italian church, had a priest who urged the ladies to tell their husbands to go to work before they turned out to be bums. I didn't hear those words since I don't go to church after coming to America, but people told me. The minister of the Protestant church, the Presbyterian, was a hundred percent with the strikers. There were others too. The Protestants were mostly with the strikers.

I tell you the IWW were the best leaders I ever had, because in the future we had other strikes but the leadership was nothing like the IWW. Carlo Tresca, he would speak to us in Italian. One time he used the Neapolitan dialect, and what he said was misinterpreted by an Italian cop who didn't understand the dialect. He thought Tresca was telling us to fight with the fist, which was not true. The police came and arrested Tresca.

Maybe they believed that story because of their own brutality. I never seen brutality like that. A lot of strikers got a cracked head. I'm lucky I never got hurt myself. But, anyway, we give and take. We threw a few stones and some bricks. The worst thing was that there was not enough regular cops. What Chief of Police Bimson did was recruit new men through the fire department and arm them with clubs and revolvers. The result of that was terrible. A strikebreaker shot Valentino Modestino when Modestino was resting on his own front porch holding his child. Another man, Vincenzo Madonna, was killed by a false striker on Ventor. After those killings we created a song so that people would never forget the deaths of those two fellows.

I think the reason we lost was we had no money. They just drained us. I'm a good example. The first time I was arrested was on Fulton Street. The shop was called Hall Mill, but it was run by Harry Doherty. I was arrested for picketing and the union had to pay five hundred dollars bail to get me out. A couple of days later I was over near Railroad Avenue. The cops came and blocked both entrances to our block. They put up a rope and all the strikers inside the rope were under arrest. There were ninety of us, and seven were taken to jail. Another five hundred dollars bail was charged to me on that incident, and another guy got hit for one thousand dollars. The third time I was arrested the union lawyer, by name of Henry Morelli, he got me out under his personal responsibility.

Even more important than the bails and fines was that strikers had to pay rent, and they didn't have money. A lot of societies paid two dollars a week for relief, but that was practically nothing if someone had children to feed and had to pay rent. Winter was up ahead, and people began to give up. We had fought very hard. Very hard. Every time we went to picket a shop, there were photographers waiting to take our pictures. The pickets they saw every day, which I was one, they put on a blacklist. Later, I couldn't even get a job in Massachusetts. After the strike, the union was completely out. We were broken-hearted—broken-hearted because we had lost our goal, humiliated because we had lost our fight.

What we stood up for in Paterson was two looms and the eight-hour day. We stood up for abolishing the child worker, for no more slavery. We stood up for respect. We said that workers should organize the same union here and in Italy and in England and all over. We didn't limit it to Europe. We said industrial workers *of the world*. We said if there was a universal strike, all production would be paralyzed. Those manufacturers, those representatives of the capitalist class, you know what they would do then? They would fall.

● *Big Bill Haywood leads sidewalk parade in Paterson, 1913.*

Irving Abrams

I became involved with the IWW at the time of the Lawrence Strike. I was living in Rochester and we hired an organizer to go to various factories like Eastman Kodak. I went along to distribute literature and agitate. We weren't very successful. Shortly afterwards, I got involved in a strike against August Brothers, a clothing cutter. The result of that was that I couldn't get hired in Rochester anymore, so I went to Utica to work.

My job at that time was being a cutter. The manufacturers would have subcontractors spread out all over the city where the wages were from eight to twelve dollars a week with very long hours. Only the clothing cutter got decent wages because cutters couldn't be replaced easily. They had to be trained, and it took a great deal of time to become an expert cutter. With the introduction of machines, that's changed to some degree, but in those days the cutters were the aristocrats of the trade.

In Utica, I became acquainted with some Italian anarchists who had a clubhouse. One day I was asked if I would go to Little Falls to help the strikers there. I went and stayed for a number of weeks. The mayor of Schenectady went too, George R. Lunn. We had no strike funds, but we managed to hold meetings and picket. The company hired armed gangsters, but we managed to avoid any violence. Wages were low everywhere at that time, but at Little Falls everything was bad: living conditions, working conditions, wages—you name it. I continued to work there until Bill Haywood came. He arrived on a Saturday. He came straight from the textile strike in Paterson.

One thing that interested me about Bill Haywood was that I had heard he was a very heavy drinker; but when he was at Utica, he refused to drink any liquor. He was an absolute teetotaler. He wore a big sombrosa hat, and while he was talking with us, he took it off to show us a scar across the top of his head. He received that when Moyers, one of his co-defendents, was brought to the Denver station during their famous trial out West. Bill went to shake hands and the police beat him with their rifles. He said he hoped to live long enough to pay the bastards back for what they did.

How the police reacted varied. I made my first public talk on the intersection of Main and Water in Rochester. I spoke on behalf of Ettor and Giovannitti. I had gone to the chief of police about getting permission to speak and he said he would not allow it. I told him if he tried to stop us, we would declare a Free Speech Fight and fill the jail with people from all over the country. He thought about that and, realizing that Rocheter was an industrial city, figured it was best to avoid any trouble and so let us go ahead. We attracted about five hundred people and collected quite a sum of money. We had other meetings afterwards and were successful in raising money for the Ettor and Giovannitti defense.

None of us were very successful in attracting Jewish people to the IWW. The background of the Jewish worker was different from the migratory elements in the IWW in the early years. The migrants moved from harvest field to harvest field, from lumber camp to lumber camp, from free speech fight to free speech fight. That was the type of activity the rank and file of the IWW was interested in. The average Jewish worker was more a home person. The major organization for them was the *Arbeter Ring*, the "Workman's Circle." It was organized on the basis that to be a member you had to belong to a union of your trade or vote for the Socialist Party. It was a fraternal benefit organization. If you openly admitted you didn't vote Socialist, you were kicked out. The only IWW material that we translated into Yiddish was the preamble. We were just a small group and had very little support. In Rochester, the local had about forty members. I doubt there were more than four or five Jewish workers. The rest were all Italians.

The struggle was very bitter in those days. I knew that when I lost my job as a cutter I would have nothing to eat until I got another job and that I would have to go to another town. One time when I was in St. Louis, I had to sleep in the IWW hall on the piano. I used magazines for a pillow and newspapers for a cover. I met an old Indian Wobbly there—Redwood Bailey, a man who had about half a dozen college degrees. He's the one who prescribed my wife's first glasses. We rarely had a dime for a can of stale rolls and coffee. He would shave me with a piece of glass because we didn't have a razor. We decided to leave St. Louis and went down to the yards. Bailey heard a ticker working incorrectly and went up to a worker and offered to correct it. When he was finished, the station head told us which gondola was going to Chicago. We left about seven or eight that night and after a few hours it started to pour. We were in that open gondola all the way and arrived soaked to the skin and very hungry. Luckily, my wife was then in Chicago, so we had somewhere to go. But that was typical of how we traveled and lived.

During the times I've been talking about, most of the IWWs I came into contact with thought of themselves as socialists, but they were socialists who didn't much believe in political action. Their goal was to build industrial unions, not a political party. They'd say casting a vote was like going to the toilet. The major problem of the day—one we never overcame—was how to keep the union going when there was no crisis. In places like Lawrence and Little Falls, despite all of our efforts, despite our great victories, the organization gradually disintegrated.

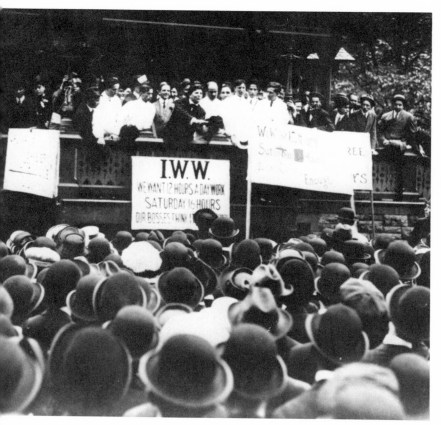

• *Joe Ettor addresses striking barbers, Union Square, New York City.*

Henry Pfaff

I came to the United States in June of 1911 after I had finished school in Europe. You were supposed to be sixteen, but I was only fifteen and had to lie. I had an awful time at sea. I couldn't eat or hold anything down. When I arrived in New York, I couldn't stand up going through customs. I had to crouch and then at the embarkation I got measles, which I had avoided all through my childhood. Somehow I managed to just pass through. I went to my father's nephew in Akron, Ohio. He was my sponsor and my guardian, so I had to stay with him. I really didn't know him in the old country, but here I had to toe the mark to him. The first day in Akron, my father's brother, who was also there, took me job hunting. I got employment in a fish hook factory, where I made lead sinkers for seven cents an hour.

I had been on the fish hook job for a couple of weeks when I met some old school chums who were working in a mirror factory making fourteen cents an hour. I didn't think they were worth more than I was, so I had them take me to their foreman. He couldn't talk to me right away, but while I was waiting a foreman from another department spied me and put me to work, which was a good thing. He was a German-speaking man, and he had another German in his department and a Hungarian. I worked there quite a while. Then, one day I made a mistake and he gave me a rubbing down which I didn't like. I quit. When I went home, my cousin was shocked. He and the old type people who thought that if you started on a job you should stick to it for life. He couldn't see that I had already changed jobs for the better. The next morning he took me to the Firestone plant where he worked, and he talked his foreman into putting me on as his helper. That didn't work out very well because I was getting eighteen cents an hour and he, a family man, was only getting half a penny more. His trouble wasn't that he was getting so little, but that I was getting nearly as much as he was. He kept grumbling, so I quit him and the shop and I went on my own.

I soon got work at the Goodrich plant in the tire curing department. I was the only kid there. The rest were grown men, big six footers. One morning I looked out the window and saw this mob of people on Main Street. They stretched for as far as you could see in both directions. I had never heard of a strike, nor had I ever really noticed the police before. We all went to the window for a look. I piped up: "What are they doing out there? Let's go out and help them." I didn't know what I was saying. The others knew and they looked down on me as though I had committed a crime. At noon, the foreman came around and told us to go out the side gate instead of the front and to come back the same way on Monday morning. The strikers had anticipated that move and had surrounded the plant. When we walked out, the strikers started marching and we fused into the line and were led down to Howard Street to a big hall where they had speakers: Haywood, Rhode Fisher, and George Trautman as well as German and Hungarian language speakers. We paid a fifty cents initiation fee. There were so many of us that they didn't have enough membership cards. They just gave us a red ribbon to pin on our lapels. I listened to Haywood for a while. The language he used was way above my comprehension, so I couldn't understand half of it. I went over to the Hungarian speaker, but he was above my level, too. So was the German. But I started to learn. A couple of days later, I was on the picket line and I saw a fellow from my department come out of the factory. I was a kid and very enthusiastic, so I ran over to him and grabbed him by the lapel. I just wanted to talk to him. I didn't understand the position he was in and the position I was in against him. The first thing I knew I was hit across my back by a club. I looked around and then I knew what a policeman was and what a policeman was for.

The main issue in that strike was that the rubber company wanted to cut wages. It went on for several weeks, but I couldn't stay. In those days young people never had enough money to last from one pay day to the next, so I went broke. I went to try my luck in Milwaukee where my mother was then living.

Eventually, I ended up working in New Brunswick, New Jersey. During World War I, I was making battery jars for use in automobilies and submarines. After about six months, I was promoted to an inspector's job, a white collar position with a fixed salary. I was doing good for myself but I was constantly fighting management on behalf of the workers. I decided to give that job up and be a regular worker again. As the war came to an end, the supervisor came around to tell us we would have to work harder if we wanted to keep our wages up. The men decided to think about organizing and I was asked to do some research.

I had no connection with any organization or union, so I decided to talk with the AF of L business agent in the community. I didn't understand the structure of the AF of L or its policy. He told me that "Hunkies" couldn't be organized. "Hunkies" to them meant any unskilled labor. Anybody who wasn't a tradesman or a craftsman was a Hunkie. I wouldn't take his say so. Because of the experience I already had with these men, I knew they could be organized and they needed to be organized.

Next I got in touch with the Socialist Labor Party representative. He promised me a speaker from New York for the following Sunday. On the strength of that, I called a meeting and we had quite a turnout, but no one, not even the local SLP representative, thought the speaker was very good. I tried to get out from under after opening the meeting, but they stuck me with being chairman. Finally, a young fellow, a member of the IWW, stood up. He had just come back from the army and he was a real radical. He was so opposed to the fighting that he had been in the stockade throughout the war. He wouldn't shoulder his gun, and he wouldn't wear a uniform. If they put a gun on his shoulder, he'd drop it. This young fellow's name was Sam Winer. He was an anarchist. After I got to know him, we used to attend doings at the Stelton Colony where the anarchists had their experimental Modern School. At this particular meeting, he had a copy of the *Industrial Worker* and the IWW preamble. I read off the preamble to the group and asked them what their pleasure was.

The men had the idea that they wanted a union that could deliver the most strike benefits. Here they were—they hadn't even paid any initiation fees or dues—and they were worried about their strike benefits! I hadn't collected any money, because I didn't think we had the right to do that if we didn't have a union. We had long discussions about these things. We got some Hungarians who were IWWs but were not working at this rubber shop to explain things.

In a short time we were able to rent a hall upstairs from the Socialist Party and call a strike. Some weeks after the strike, one of our Polish members got into an argument with a guy who had scabbed on us. The Polish fellow pulled a knife and stabbed the scab. We went over to the jail to find out about the case and then went back to our hall. When we got there, we saw that the Socialist Party offices had been broken into. Their door was smashed and furniture and literature were all over the floor. We thought some local hoodlums had done it. We went upstairs to see whether we had been broken into, but evidently they didn't know about our hall. Anyhow, we decided I should go to New York to see the American Civil Liberties Union about the fellow worker in jail.

I arrived in New York before office hours and went over to the IWW hall. As I got near the building, I saw the secretary coming to open up. Well, we didn't need any keys. The door was broken, and all our furniture, typewriters, books, and other things were smashed. We still didn't know what had happened, so we went down to get the morning newspaper. There were big headlines about raids on the IWW all over the country. These were the famous Palmer Raids. I decided to go ahead with my original plan to see Roger Baldwin at the ACLU. I told him about our situation. He said that given things as they were, it was better for our man in New Brunswick not be connected with the IWW. He advised me to do nothing, to let it go as a personal fight and in a few months the guy would get paroled. If we made it political by connecting it to the IWW, they could crucify him. We followed Baldwin's advice and it worked out like I thought it would.

Ever since then, 1919, I've been an IWW member. Joining in 1913 didn't make me a real member because I just paid initiation and that was it. I never learned much until I came to New Brunswick and started that union. Before that I was like any other common working man who is mainly concerned with getting more

money. The IWW gave me a vision of how we could change America—from a profit motivated society to a cooperative society where no man needs to work for another for his livelihood, but all cooperate together to provide necessities. That was the greatest appeal for me. I never had a penchant for property or money. The vision we had was that everyone would have to do a necessary share of social production and everyone would receive all the necessities without the need for money. And we wouldn't have to work eight hours a day. We would eliminate all useless work and all work that is detrimental. We would center our collective efforts on useful things. Perhaps we would have to start out with four hours a day in the beginning until we got things straightened out. Then we could cut it down to three and before long, to two.

I'm inclined to believe that the IWW saved my life. If I hadn't been swept into it, I would be six feet under the ground long since. I would have probably worked myself to death like a lot of others did, like my brother-in-law who passed several years ago. He was a good slave. He kept on trying to amass wealth and to live for money, whereas I have not. Money was never my god. I have learned, day by day, that my nature is inquisitive, not acquisitive. I could not have gained the knowledge I have gotten through the IWW for all the wealth in the world.

Vaino Konga

Researchers have shown that eighty percent of the Finns who came to the United States migrated from the provinces of Oll and Wasa. These are agrarian areas, so the people had few industrial or urban skills. They had to go into iron ore mines because no skill was required. It also happens that Minnesota ore country looks, to a great extent, a lot like Finland, which made it attractive. The Finns soon became part of the Western Federation of Miners. They played a leading role in the big strike of 1907. Another major strike came in 1916 and that's when the IWW took hold. This 1916 strike was very violent, involving company gunmen and all that.

My father worked in various western states and Michigan before finding more permanent work in Waukegan, Illinois, in 1905. He was a molder and became a journeyman in the foundries. As soon as he got some money together, he sent for us and we settled in Kenosha, which is sixteen miles north of Waukegan on the Wisconsin side. That's where I went to school and spent my childhood.

I met my first IWW in 1917 when I attended a Socialist Sunday school instead of going to a church school. A year later I subscribed to the *Industrialiste*, because my dad wanted us to have that news. The *Industrialiste* had just started up, but there were predecessors like the *Socialiste* which supported Finnish workers on the Mesabi and Vermillion Ranges in Minnesota. You must understand that the Finnish language is vastly different from Indo-European languages, so Finns had a very difficult time learning English. They had their own press for a long time. They were not like the Germans, the Italians, or the Swedes, who could pick up English more easily.

The Finns brought the cooperative movement with them from Europe. Cooperatives had been very popular in Scandinavia and Finland for decades. When the Finns went up to northern Minnesota and northern Michigan, a store would open up and try to take advantage of their isolation. The Finns said to heck with that noise. They'd band together and open a cooperative store, which resulted in refunds, lower prices, and better quality. They were used to working as a community. Since they didn't have bulldozers to clear stumps, they had to depend on a combination of some sticks of dynamite and a lot of physical manpower and womanpower. Alcoholism was a big problem, just as it had been in the old country, so there was a strong temperance movement from which many socialist and labor clubs emanated. These organizations tended to drift toward the more radical groups like the IWW.

The community halls run by the Finns proved to be critical to the development of the labor movement. Some of the halls housed the local IWW branch. If there was a strike or talk of a strike, the hall was where we would gather, because you couldn't risk a meeting at the place of work. All the halls had educational lectures and quite a few had libraries. People in the halls liked the IWW sense of humor and the IWW songs. We printed the songbook in Finnish, and some of the more comical tunes became very popular.

Wobbly influence on the Finns was extensive. For example, at one time the IWW organized the entire town of Crosby, Minnesota. Crosby was a little mining town about a hundred miles west of Duluth. At most of the boarding houses, where you also got your meals, you had to have an IWW card to be a regular guest. You could get an individual meal without being a member, but you could not be a boarder. That was pretty basic: you had to have the red card right at the place where you filled your stomach.

Speaking of food reminds me that there was a hotel and restaurant workers union in Duluth where the majority of the members were women. The IWW always tried to involve women as much as possible. If there was a strike, the women were there fighting alongside the men. I'm not talking about making coffee. During one strike at a newspaper, my wife picked up a gas canister they had thrown at us and tossed it back.

I began working when I was fourteen and I joined the IWW one year later. The way it happened was that I was working in a restaurant and all my friends were IWWs. After I studied the literature and went to some activities, I joined up. Later I worked on railroads and construction jobs, and I did quite a bit of lumbering, too. I have lumbered redwoods in California, cordwood in Massachusetts and Maine, and various woods in Michigan and Minnesota. I was never one of those guys who believed in this muscleman-health stuff, but I did like to work outside. I thought it was better for my lungs, so I never looked for work in factories. But after I was blacklisted and during the Depression, I was forced to take what I could get in lots of places: Detroit, Duluth, Kenosha. I even got some work in an automobile factory, but I found that kind of work very monotonous.

I happened to be at the farewell meeting of 1921 in Chicago. That was for the men convicted in the famous trial of 1918. During the time appeals were being made, quite a few got out on bond, but the decision had finally come down that they all had to return to Leavenworth Penitentiary. The farewell event was held on a Sunday at the Troop Street hall. There were hundreds of people listening to speakers in many different languages. The next day some of us went down to the attorney's office to see the fellows off when the marshals came. I was too much of a youngster to fully comprehend what was happening. Different men took it differently. Some had big smiles, no matter what they felt inside. A lot seemed to think that this was part of the struggle and they had to go through with it. They knew that labor leaders in other

• *Outdoor rally for incarcerated IWWs.*

countries had been framed on all kinds of pretenses. Naturally, there was an air of sadness. At the same time, there was the feeling—and I recall it very well—that this is not the end. The men going to prison felt that the members who were on the outside would carry on the work they had initiated.

I think the educational force of the IWW has never been fully appreciated. At one time, the IWW simultaneously published newspapers and leaflets in twelve to fifteen languages. I was familiar with the Russian paper, the Bulgarian paper, the Swedish paper, the Finnish paper, the Spanish paper, and the French paper. I've met people who were in the IWW who tell me that they learned their ABCs of labor and their ABCs of living from the IWW. Although we never became a major force in industry, we definitely showed the way for the CIO. Don't think it's an accident that the United Auto Workers adopted "Solidarity Forever" as their main song.

I'm still an IWW. I believe the IWW is one of the most democratic organizations ever conceived and that it is a union with a vision. I still foresee the day when we shall have some organization very much close to it that will create a world where we produce for use instead of profit. I'm a retiree now. Looking back, I'm content with what I did. I suppose if I had been more of an individualist, if I had gone out and strived for myself, I would be much further ahead economically. But I have the innermost feeling that I tried to do the right thing when I decided to better, not only my own personal position, but the position of others. My wife and I still believe that for those who are in industry organization is the salvation and that the organization of our class is the salvation of the human race. If we leave things to the powers that be, they will surely drop the atom bombs and destroy the world.

AUTO-WORKERS

> *I traveled extensively with the IWWs and came to know them as warm-hearted people who, it seemed to me even then, had higher ideals than some of the men who ran our banks and were the elders in the church. A hungry man was always welcome under that railroad bridge; not only was he offered food, but there he could feel that he was an equal with everyone. And almost always, these drifters left the area cleaner than they had found it.*
> —Justice° William O. Douglas
> *Go East, Young Man: The Early Years*

TIMBERBEASTS

Most timber workers were either native-born Americans or immigrants from Northern Europe. While their pay was good relative to that of other laborers, work conditions were brutal and unsafe. The guerilla-style, point-of-production approach of the IWW proved to be ideally suited to an industry dependent on a multitude of scattered camps and saw mills where order was maintained by a local foreman. Within a year of the formation of the IWW, there were eight hundred members in the Seattle local, and within two years there were functioning units in over half a dozen American and Canadian cities. The largest of these was in Portland which had two thousand dues-paying members.

In 1907 under the leadership of Fred Heslewood and Joe Ettor, the Portland Wobblies mounted a drive for a nine hour day to be paid at $2.50 per day minimum. Every mill in the area was soon closed, and the action captured the imagination of lumber workers in the Pacific Northwest. The strike ended with mixed economic gains, but many of the affected firms voluntarily granted some of the key strike demands a short time later in hopes of forestalling further growth of the IWW.

A significant aspect of the Portland strike was the women's

• *Pacific Northwest.*

brigade organized by IWW Nina Wood. Similar brigades would be seen in the West wherever lumber or mine workers had established families. The women did not limit themselves to support work, but actively engaged in picketing which led to physical confrontations with strikebreakers and law officers. In one Washington strike, a women's brigade announced it had spent an afternoon cutting five hundred wood switches to use on the back of any scabs who dared to test their picket line.

Two years after the Portland strike, Spokane became the site for the first major free speech fight. The struggle lasted for four months, and thousands of IWWs, including James P. Thompson, Frank Little, and Gurley Flynn participated. Eight consecutive editors of the local IWW paper were arrested, and the IWW hall was raided several times. But with six hundred Wobblies in jail and a national call to flood the city with more free speechers, the city fathers decided to end the struggle. On March 5, 1910, the mayor announced that street speaking would no longer be prohibited, that all IWWs would be released unconditionally, that IWW offices would no longer be disturbed, and that *The Industrial Worker* could publish unmolested. In return, the IWW would drop its damage suits against the municipality and refrain from public speaking until the prohibiting ordinance was officially rescinded, an action that took place four days later by unanimous vote of the city council.

Free speech fights consumed considerable IWW energy in the following years, but after 1915 the policy in lumber, as in agriculture, officially shifted "from the soapbox to the job." Dues-paying membership fluctuated between ten thousand and twenty thousand a year between 1916 and 1919, but Wobbly power was considerably greater than even these impressive numbers indicate. Getting dues collected regularly from isolated camps scattered in remote areas would have been a formidable task for any union, and the IWW was never a model of bureaucratic efficiency. What its organizers could do much better than collect dues regularly was spread ideas, and the irrepressible idea of the late teens was direct action.

A dramatic test of direct action came in Everett, a city of some thirty-five thousand inhabitants located on Puget Sound. Its port was a strategic center for shipping cut lumber, and its hiring halls recruited men for operations in the interior. On May 1, 1916, over four hundred of the town's shingle cutters went on strike. Sheriff Donald McRae began to arrest pickets, and the local sent out a national call for assistance. Although the shingle workers belonged to the AFL, which did not respond to their appeal, the IWW sent

James Rowan from Seattle to organize a solidarity campaign. As soon as Rowan got up to speak on a soapbox, Sheriff McRae arrested him and a free speech fight was on. After several other attempts to speak in public had failed in spite of considerable local support, October 30th was set as the date for a major effort. On that day a contingent of forty-one Wobblies went to Everett on the regular passenger ferry from Seattle. Before they even had a chance to leave the dock area, they were surrounded by a sheriff's posse. Shortly thereafter they were taken to a park on the outskirts of town where they were severely beaten. About a week later another two hundred fifty Wobblies made the same trip, determined to

• *Upright shingle machine, Seaside Mill, Everett, Washington, 1911.*

hold a public meeting at all costs. This group was met by a drunken sheriff and deputies who shot into the ferry as it tried to dock. Some of the Wobblies shot back, and before the boat could pull away there were at least five dead, six missing, and twenty-seven wounded Wobblies. On the shore, a deputy was mortally wounded, a lumber company official was dead and twenty-four were wounded. The Everett Free Speech Fight had become the Everett Massacre. The immediate aftermath was that seventy-four Wobblies, rather than law enforcement personnel, were put on trial, the typical IWW experience in which the victim was treated as the criminal. The murder trial ended with a spectacular legal victory in 1917 which served to further fuel the determination of lumber workers to achieve long-sought basic reforms.

The unruly lumber operators had never been able to work together harmoniously, but the threat of the IWW brought forth the Lumberman's Protective Association, which promptly raised half a million dollars for union-busting activities. The sum was easily raised because of the astronomical profits made possible by World War I. The war also allowed the owners to call upon the national government for assistance in protecting an industry vital to the war effort. One of the centerpieces of the anti-IWW effort was the Loyal Legion of Loggers and Lumbermen, a company union organized under the direct guidance of Col. Brice P. Disque of the U.S. Army Signal Corps. Claiming the IWW strikers were unpatriotic, the owners dubbed them "Imperial Wilhelm's Warriors." Vigilante violence, government raids, the use of army draftees to cut timber, and the jailing of strikers were tactics used to test the determination of the IWW. Col. Disque even granted the eight-hour day and other IWW demands in an effort to dissuade lumber workers from organizing. Such concessions angered the majority of owners, who had always depended on brute force. Their intractable refusal to bargain collectively would lead to many violent incidents, none more infamous than the 1919 shootout at Centralia.

What the lumber owners eventually realized was that elimination of a few IWW organizers or even destabilization of an IWW center did not have the same devastating effect as in mining regions, where the facilities were large and stationary. Lumber operations were so mobile and decentralized that once consensus had been forged upon fundamental demands and workers became familiar with direct action tactics, the question was no longer *whether* lumberjacks would improve their economic prospects, but by how much.

The oral histories of Irving Hanson, Jack Miller,[1] and Nels

Peterson concentrate on the often bloody IWW organizing drives in the Northwest, rather than on day-to-day conditions. These Wobblies previously had labored in mining and agriculture and after their years in the forests went on to other kinds of work. In this respect, they illustrate the futility of trying to pigeonhole most laborers of that era into a specific work category or industry. What they have to say about the life of the timberbeast will be amplified in later testimonies by George Hodin and Tom Scribner. Violet Miller, not herself a timber worker, embellishes these accounts of the lumber wars with a rare glimpse of an IWW family that was not particularly militant. She also speculates on how IWW thinking about sexism relates to the kind of women's issues she encountered in the 1970s.

Irving Hanson

I first heard about socialism in 1912, when I was sixteen. A friend of mine, my brother, and I had left Iowa on a freight train for Arizona because we heard there was a lot of work out there. Of course, the whole country had heard the same thing and there weren't too many jobs. We heard some work was available in the Mascot Mine at Dos Cabezas. To get there we had to wade up the Salt River for about thirty miles and then walk cross country. We ran out of food and had to shoot some rabbits and quail to survive. When we got there, my friend, who was a miner, got a job right away, but my brother and I had to wait around for a couple of weeks. We lived off rabbits, thanks to our .22 rifle. Finally, we got hired. That's when I met an old miner named Hickory. I'm pretty sure he belonged to the Western Federation of Miners. He was also an actor. At lunchtime, he would arrange candles around a pile of muck and get up and put on a show. He would give us lectures on socialism, unionism, and various other subjects. He was quite well educated. Some of the Mexican miners couldn't talk much English, but I think they got something out of it too.

I didn't join the IWW until 1919, when I was doing harvest work in the East. I stayed until 1923 and shortly after that I went into farming. I didn't want to work for others anymore. It hasn't been much of an occupation, but you don't have a boss looking down your neck. When I joined the IWW, there were about four hundred men about to get on a freight. That was a good place for organizers to make contact. Later I transferred to the lumberjacks. We could transfer to a number of unions. That was one of our selling points to recruits. I was also a reader of the *Appeal to Reason*, and I had met Eugene Debs in Missoula, where my brother was secretary in a union. I drifted into reading socialist, left-wing, and philosophical literature. It seemed a logical answer to a rather troubled world.

Portland was a center for the Northwest lumber industry, and the Portland hall was a center for the IWW. Seattle had a share in it, too. Our secretary, P.J. Wild, had a Ph.D. in Economics and History from a university in Europe. We had another Ph.D., Dr.

Chapman, who was no longer desirable at the agricultural school in Eugene. He gave us lectures twice a week in economics and sociology. We had a good chance to learn, and we had a fine library to take books from.

Talking together we got the idea for job delegates. The procedure was to furnish a person with some cards, stamps, and maybe a hundred dollars, and send him out to the camps. We got hundreds of volunteers and enjoyed very good success. The lumber companies were very worried about these job delegates. They were not paid organizers, not professionals, just lumberjacks. The companies employed goons and gunmen to stop them. Some delegates were killed and many were beaten up. I almost got shot myself one time.

We had a lot of trouble with hijackers on our trains. They would go looking for organizers, because an organizer might have a thousand dollars or more of IWW funds in a satchel. We had to form an anti-hijacking "flying squad." The leader of this group in our area was an unusual man. He had been born in the slums of Chicago and had followed the harvest from Texas to Saskatchewan for twenty years. He knew the ropes from A to Z. He was a very concerned and organized person. He would travel with three or four other guys, and he had a sawed-off shotgun down one leg of a loose pair of pants. I never saw him in action, but he was a very formidable type of person. What I did see him doing was recruiting, talking to men about the advantages of unionism. He was completely self-educated, but he had read a lot of books. I think he knew as much about economics and sociology as those Ph.D.s. That was the kind of guy who was captain of the flying squad.

Another time in Portland, we formed an IWW police force. This was during a big strike when we wanted to keep the guys from spending their money on booze. Four hundred men were organized with armbands and captains, with about three to four thousand loggers as backups. They went to those speakeasies and bootleg joints that they had patronized for years. They filled the place up and had signs reading, "Stop Selling This Poison." The proprietors were very glad to shut down under the pressure of all those men. The Women's Christian Temperance Union got wind of the action. Portland was dry at that time, so they gave the IWW a lot of publicity. We got into the major newspapers. As far as I can remember, it was the only favorable publicity we ever had.

Another unusual incident took place in Astoria. We had a free speech fight going, and they had a vigilante group of about fifty, including the city law officers. They had put sixty people in jail for setting up soap boxes, and we had about four hundred loggers ready to follow. Astoria wasn't very big at that time, so we decided to hold a free speech parade. We painted a bunch of signs in red: "Free Speech," "Free America," "Freedom"—all that kind of stuff. I used a big house painter's brush and a gallon of fresh paint, which I smeared on heavily. While we were parading, the vigilantes stopped us. They were a minority in terms of numbers, and we had a kind of street fracas. There wasn't much rough stuff, but we saw that the red paint was still fresh, so we tried to smear the uniforms of the police and the suits of the businessmen as much as possible. A kind of carnival spirit developed. You see, we wanted to go to jail, and we got our wish. While we were waiting for trial, the overzealous city dads set up a criminal syndicalist ordinance. Our attorney came up from Portland and told them a few facts of legal life, and they cut us loose.

We were all interested in the Russian Revolution. During the civil war, the United States undertook to furnish Kolchak with supplies for the White Army he was raising in Siberia. The workers in Seattle and Portland refused to cooperate. They didn't want that ship going over there, so they picketed it. There was ammunition and other kinds of explosives that made it a bit dangerous for the

• *Interior of saw mill.*

Seattle waterfront. That ship, the *S.S. Delight*, never sailed. The
United States had some troops over there, and I feel our opposition
may have helped keep the government from intervening around
Vladivostok. Anyway, Kolchak was defeated. I hope that what we
did helped.

Our basic approach was not to talk about revolution too much.
We talked about immediate gains, union gains. That was the main
pitch when you went into a lousy old camp where they were
working ten hours for low wages under conditions demanding
immediate improvement. The loggers could readily understand
the need for immediate change. Meanwhile, the goal of an ultimate
socialist society was stated quite plainly in our literature. We
figured the people who were interested would read up on it.
Another place we talked about socialism was in the song book,
which I still have. One song that kind of appealed to me had these
verses:

> *We hate this rotten system more than any mortals do;*
> *Our aim is not to patch it up, but build it all anew.*
> *And what we'll have for government when we are through*
> *Is one big industrial union.*
>
> *Hurrah! Hurrah! We're going to paint it red.*
> *Hurrah! Hurrah! The way is clear ahead.*
> *We're going to have shop democracy and liberty and bread.*
> *In one big industrial union.*

A lot of the other tunes have had more impact, but for some reason
that one got to me. The police used the verses as evidence in trials.
They'd claim that "we're going to paint it red" meant you wanted
to overthrow the government.

What we wanted was a socialist society. My brother was
involved in the IWW, too. His ideas weren't always close to mine,
but in general they were much the same. It's not a personal idea.
It's all part of a world happening. We're finding out all over that
building a new social structure is not a simple task, but I think
some people in the world are going in the right direction. I don't
feel pessimistic at all.

Jack Miller

The big fight of 1916 developed in Everett, Washington, where the shingle workers were on strike. The trademark of that work was severed fingers. Workers had to maneuver a block with the right hand and the shingle with the left in front of a fast moving blade. The shingle weavers had a small union of a few hundred men, and they had gone on strike because their wages had been cut.

The IWW didn't have a branch office in Everett, but it responded to the call of the shingle workers for help. James Rowan, who had been organizing in Minnesota, was among the first to arrive. When he got up to read the Industrial Relations Commission Report, a document published by the government of the United States, he was taken from his soap box and told he could not speak. Now the religious people could talk and any idiot could say the moon was made of green cheese, but it was a "no-no" to talk about the plight of the shingle weavers. You see Everett was not built by pioneers; it was planned as a workplace. The timbermen's association ran the town and had Sheriff Don McRae doing their dirty work.

The IWW decided to send a group of speakers from Seattle on October 30th. We took the regular ferry, and were met at the docks by Sheriff McRae. He told us, "To hell with the constitution; you're in Everett now." The word arrest was never used, but they put us in cars and took us to Beverly Park on the outskirts of town. He had a hundred men lined up on each side of us, his regular deputies and volunteers from the Commercial Club. If we had tried to make a break for it, they would have shot us. What they made us do was run a gauntlet. They were armed with every kind of cudgel imaginable—sawed billiard cues, billy clubs, small baseball bats, brass knuckles, pistol butts. As you ran, they clubbed at you.

I was the fourth to go through. Other guys had tried holding their coats over their hands but that wasn't much protection. I tried a new tactic of ducking and weaving. I managed to get past the first and second pair. I also slipped past the third, but someone grabbed me by the necktie. Then I felt a blow on my head and

● *The Verona, 1910.*

another under my eye. That's all I can tell you because I'm not
sure I was fully conscious after that; I was what they call out on
your feet. Somehow I got to the end of the line. I had a small scalp
wound and bruises that lasted for months, and my eye was completely blackened. I didn't consider this much. One of the IWWs
was crippled for life; his arm was pulled from his shoulder so badly
that he could never do heavy lifting again. There were lots of con-
cussions and fractures. We were just left out there. We had brought
very little money with us because we thought the sheriff might
rob us, but there was small change. We put the worse injured on
the first interurban car. The rest of us made it back as best we
could. I caught a freight. Thirty-one of us had to receive treatment
at the Seattle City Hospital.

We knew that the next time we went to Everett, it would have
to be in much larger numbers and in daylight. Our trip would be
advertised extensively. We had so much support after the beatings
that one minister in Everett, with the consent of his congregation,
wanted us to come to a park to hold a big public meeting. I'm
not sure how many responded because we took the regular
passenger run and we paid the regular fare. There were about two
hundred and fifty of us and an overflow of about another fifty

who had to wait for the next boat, the *Calista*. We sang all the way—"Hold the Fort," "Solidarity," and all the other songs.

I was below deck as we came in for the landing and starting to come forward when I heard a shot. Sheriff McRae was standing there, one hand in the air and one near the butt of his pistol. His coat was thrown back so that his belly stuck out way over the belt. He yelled out, "Who's your leader?" Someone answered, "We're all leaders." He said, "You can't land here." Someone else yelled, "The hell we can't." Immediately after that there was a volley fired from the dock. The boat had made a port landing, and there was so much panic with people rushing to the opposite side that the boat listed and many were pitched into the water. I don't know how many were hit in the volley, but the firing was indiscriminate.

My first impulse was to run, but I realized that would attract fire, so I walked down to a lower deck. In case bullets started coming my way, I stacked up two sacks of coal for shelter. Two armed men approached me. One was Ben Legs. He was full or part Indian. These men had the only pistols I actually saw that day. I told them not to waste their ammunition. They should watch the outer edge of the dock. Men stationed there could cross fire the boat lengthwise and every bullet could strike someone. If a deputy showed his head, they should discourage him.

But they had a better idea. Instead of guarding the dock, they located the engineer hiding behind the boiler and told him to pull the boat out before we were all killed. I couldn't actually hear what they told him. There was too much shooting, screaming and shouting. I saw Ben Legs point the pistol, and he told me afterwards he had said, "Buddy, it would be pretty hard to miss you from here." So they forced the engineer to go out and back the boat away. I've been told that once we got moving, the IWWs found the captain in his quarters, which was just behind the wheelhouse. He was hiding behind a safe with a mattress over his head. They forced him to take over the wheel at gunpoint. All you had to do was look at the pictures of that boat afterwards, and you could see he hadn't been behind the wheel when the firing began. There were at least seventeen bullet holes in the pilot house. The odd thing about all this is that even though I was a participant, I didn't see very much.

On the trip back we saw the *Calista* and warned them about what happened and they turned around. Three men were already dead, two of them dying on the way back to Seattle, and we never found out how many were drowned. The militia met us at the old Coleman Dock when we got back to Seattle. They marched us to the public safety building and took us through a tunnel to elevators that brought us to the top floor. There were so many of us in there that there wasn't room to lie down. We had to make a system where men would lie partially on top of one another in order to get some rest. The diet we had was bread and coffee once a day. That lasted three days and then we decided to retaliate by "building a battleship." This was IWW parlance for doing unpleasant things for the benefit of the jailer.

Since there were no tin cups or bars to bang, about twenty of us went into the center of the room, locked our arms and jumped as high as we could. The aggregate weight, which was about a ton and a half, came down in one spot. Buildings are not made to sustain such abuse and it wasn't long until almost everyone was in the circle. People who were observing from outside have told me since that the building began to sway. The jailers threatened to turn a hose on us, but we said that would make it easier to form a hole for the water to run through. Then they said we were making it bad for our comrades in the hospital on the floor below who might even be dying. Someone replied that if those fellow workers heard us fighting, they were likely to get well and come on up and join us. No one would die as long as we were still fighting. The chief of police came up and got the same sort of replies. Finally Mayor Gill came and promised better food and some blankets. The meals did get a lot better, but the blankets were a mixed blessing as they were infested.

I didn't keep a diary, but I think it was about two days later that the prosecuting attorney came in. We were never taken before a grand jury and property indicted. We were charged from information provided by the prosecutor. He decided to charge forty-one of us with first degree murder. He spoke very softly. I walked up close to the doorway and asked him to repeat himelf. He mumbled, "First degree murder." "Oh, hell," I said, "I thought it was something serious." But the reactions among us varied. We had a cross section in there. One guy fainted from shock, and there was general pandemonium for a while. Later, they made the same charge on another thirty-three of us. They stopped at that number because the jail couldn't house any more prisoners.

The ones charged with murder were moved to the brand new and escape-proof Snohomish county jail in Everett. What they fed us there looked like the swill a farmer throws to his hogs. We had to build another battleship. We threw the stew on those fine new walls, and we were able to force the cell doors open. We couldn't do anything with the tank doors, but we bent the cell frames so they could not be latched properly. The fellows downstairs took all the levers from the upper locking system and bent them out of shape. That cost $980 to repair. I told McCullough, the man who had since been elected sheriff, that he could have bought a lot of good food for what that battleship had cost him.

We demanded separate trials and for the first case, I was among the twenty-five witnesses called. My function was to verify that we had had to use a pistol to get the engineer to back the boat away from the dock. The crew had simply deserted their posts and left us at the mercy of McRae. The prosecution never presented any evidence as to how the deputies had been shot. There were no rifles on board the ship. We had some pistols, so you can bet your life that if the deputies had been hit by pistol fire, there would have been evidence to that effect.

We received a lot of support during the trial, which was held back in Seattle. The Kerensky Revolution had already occurred in Russia and there were lots of emigres who were thinking of going back. On May 1, a large group went to Mt. Pleasant Cemetary to pay tribute to the boys who had been killed at Everett, and then they came to serenade us. We didn't know about this until we heard voices singing in the distance. As they got closer, we realized the song was "The Internationale" being sung in four different languages. Besides the Russians, there were a lot of Germans and Australians. Some of our prisoners were Australian, too. Well, the people outside would sing a revolutionary song in one language or another and we woud reply with an IWW song. That went on until dark. It was one of the most thrilling days of my life. Here we were incarcerated on charges of first degree murder, and there were more than a thousand people outside the jail singing to us. We were in a revolutionary upsurge. Four days after that singing, the verdict of "not guilty" came in on Tom Tracy, the first defendent. The charges against the rest of us were soon dropped.

There was a conspiracy to stop the IWW even before the United States got into World War I and before there was a Bolshevik Revolution. The lumber barons were worried. They thought that if they broke the shingle weavers' strike, they could break other unions. The longshoremen had just been defeated after a long strike. They didn't make any bones about their goal of destroying unions. Our motto was, "We have nothing to lose but our chains." Look at it this way: when conditions and wages are below subsistence, you lose if you continue to work. When you only have part-time work offered, it isn't much of a hardship to be on strike.

Lumberjacks have got to be the most independent of workers. A lumberjack is a big man with a Paul Bunyan complex. But between the time of the shooting at Everett on November 5, 1916, and mid-summer of 1917, we organized those lumberjacks in Idaho, Oregon, Washington, Northern California, and parts of Montana. Some fifty thousand lumberjacks went on strike at the call of the IWW, and there was not one single act of violence. No one ever crossed the picket lines and no logger remained in a camp where an IWW could reach him to tell him the strike was on. After that walkout, the timberbeast was on the way out.

We came up with all kinds of tricks to reach the loggers. One time we pretended to be tobacco salesmen. The idea was that every logger chewed regular tobacco, plug tobacco, or Copenhagen. There was very little smoking. First, there wouldn't be time to light up a pipe, and it was dangerous. So we got some choice cakes of Plum tobacco, which was the most popular brand, and cut them into small pieces that we wrapped in nice tinfoil. Our organizer would go into a camp with his tobacco about the time the men were coming in for their meal break. He would pass out his "samples" and then he'd go into the kitchen and take out the strike posters he had brought with him and put them wherever he could. He would also go into the bunkhouse and contact anyone he knew had a red card. We broke into quite a few camps that way.

Recruitment and direct action remained strong even after the United States entered the war in February of 1917. The One Big

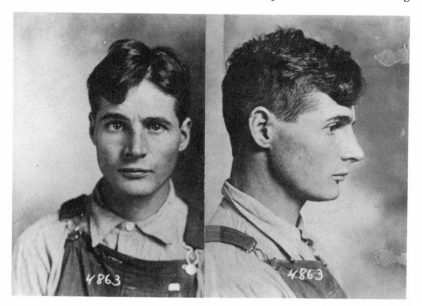

• *Police mug shot of Jack Miller, 1916.*

Union was going well in western Canada, and our membership was growing. Everett had been a terrible legal defeat for the lumber bosses. They had thought they could railroad us one after another for being violent. Now they had to find somthing new. They began to accuse us of being pro-German and of helping the Kaiser by going on strike. They charged us with wanting to overthrow the government. The profits involved were enormous because a lot of spruce was needed to build airplanes, and contractors were paid at cost plus. Even though the spruce tree is found wherever timber grows in Oregon, Washington, Idaho, and some parts of Montana, J.D. Ryan, a big shot in the Milwaukee Railroad who was head of spruce production, thought that production could only be profitably cut on the Olympia Penninsula. He built a branch line of the Milwaukee to haul it out. I think the main reason was that he thought the Loyal Legion of Lumbermen and Loggers would do the work and there would be little contact with the IWW. Well, our activities interfered with deals like that, so they had to have the government come in. They drafted people into the Spruce Division, and they supported the 4-Ls, which they had formed in the first place.

What hurt us the most was the defense trials they kept putting us through. We had to continuously raise money for the trials instead of organizing. The Mesabi Iron Range flared up again and we couldn't respond efficiently, because we had to keep the organization going.

I have often been asked if the sacrifice of the five known dead at Everett and all the beatings, jailings, and other outrages were worth it. My answer is "yes." The depth of principle in the IWW was just incredible. One time an escaped parolee from Pennsylvania was offered the remission of his time if he would be a prosecution witness against the IWW. He refused. When they came to take him back, we tried to cheer him up by singing. That was such an emotional moment. To think that a man would be willing to sacrifice five or six years in prison rather than forsake his ideals.

In the senior citizens' movement of which I am now a part, I find a new chance of being useful, to make life more pleasant. They have given me a new nickname, "Jack the Agitator." Even the mayor called me that in one of his speeches. I'm proud of that. To agitate means to stir up. That's what I do. I still believe the IWW has the only and final solution to our problems. It taught us that the most fundamental thing is that if we take a clump of clay from a mudbank and put in on a potter's wheel, we can make it into a beautiful vase. That can only be accomplished by the magic of human effort. When human effort shall be the most important thing we have, the most precious of all things, not a commodity but a voluntary service, then and only then, will we be free.

We also said we had no leaders. We meant just that. That didn't mean we didn't recognize that someone might be a better speaker or organizer or better at this or that, but they had no authority. No one ever sent an IWW anywhere to do anything. When I say the organization sent someone, that's just a convenient way of speaking. But it would be a defeat against myself and all our purposes if anything I have said makes people think that I believe or that we believed among ourselves that we were all saints in the IWW, even in our attitude to our cause. We were not. We were ordinary men and women. We had the weaknesses and appetites that all other men and women have. That we were so ordinary is what is important. Ordinary people did all those remarkable things that history shows us the IWW accomplished.

Nels Peterson

I joined the IWW in 1913 or 1914. I'm not sure of the exact year or date. I was working in the harvest fields. We would start down by the Texas border of Oklahoma and work north to Canada. They'd arrest you in those little towns and fine you for vagrancy or just rob you outright. It was a racket. I experienced it myself many times. I remember one time I was picked up with a bunch of guys in Hutchinson, Kansas, and fined thirty days or twenty-five dollars. I had been working in Oklahoma and had about forty dollars rolled up in my sleeve that they didn't find, but I refused to pay. They put us all in a great big old cell in the city hall. There was a tall ceiling and you could stand on top of the cell and hear the judge pounding his gavel in the room directly above us. One day while we were in there, we tore out one of the cell doors, and when he began to pound the gavel, he crashed through the ceiling. They told us to get out of town and never come back.

This other time, we got picked up on the weekend and got our trial that Monday. We had a lawyer in them days. That was before we quit having them. "On top of that building is a statue," he told the court. "That statue represents liberty. These men deserve their liberty." Oh, he went on and on. In the meantime, the judge fell asleep. The "cutor"—that was the prosecutor, we called him "cutor"—woke him up, and the judge says, "Twenty-five dollars or thirty days in jail." And we stayed there the full thirty days.

Still another time in jail came when I went to shuck corn in Quincy, Illinois. They picked us all up and took us to the jail without making any charges. I was wondering what was going on, when an old-timer said to wait until Tuesday. "That's election day," he says. "You'll see then." The day arrived, and they brought one of those old fashioned three-seaters to the jail, a kind of bus, and hauled us to different precinct stations and told us who to vote for. When we were done, they took us to the train, gave us a dollar apiece, and told us to scram. That's how they treated us. We were up against that kind of stuff all the time. We had to get organized.

Fellows who didn't understand about unions we'd call a "Mr.

Mr. Block

He Works in the Woods

Block." The song says, "His head is made of lumber, and solid as a rock. He's a common worker, and his name is Mr. Block." He's so dumb he thinks he can be President some day and when he climbs the golden ladder he asks St. Peter if he can meet the "Astorbilts" and "John D. Rockefell." Old Pete tells him, "You'll meet *them* down below."

For a time I kept the books of the IWW in Everett and looked after the hall. I had many experiences with people who thought they could bribe us. One day, during a time when the longshoremen were on strike, I was working at a desk. A fellow comes in and asks how much it would be to stop the strike. I told him I couldn't stop the strike if I wanted to. I was the secretary, but I didn't have a vote in that matter. I informed him that he could speak to the strike committee, but that he shouldn't make that kind of offer because they'd throw him out on his heels. He couldn't figure it out. He went outside and stared through the window at me. I looked back. I could see he was pretty mad. I thumbed my nose at him. That kind of thing happened quite often. They thought if they could bribe one man they could settle things, which they could not. The secretary didn't have any power, just a membership.

I was still working for the IWW in Everett at the time of the massacre. That morning me and another fellow walked down there and tried to get on the dock. They had a rope stretched across the street, which was against the law, too, but that's big business for you—they do any damn thing they want to. The man that was on guard at that rope I knew right well. He was superintendent of the Ferry Baker Saw Mill. When we saw that he had a rifle over his shoulder, we knew there was going to be trouble. We walked away and got below the boat depot to a beach. We waited there, and sure enough bullets started flying when the *Verona* came in.

I don't know how many they shot. Nobody knows. Lots of them went overboard. Some of them jumped and some of them fell. It was terrible. And they tried to tell us later that they didn't shoot anybody in the water. Well, I know better, and this other fellow, too. I wish he were alive, but he's gone a long time now. One man was swimming toward shore. We got about halfway, and we run down the beach to see if we could find a boat to go out and help him. But they got him. Bullets flew all around him and come my way too. It was no use. You couldn't do anything. The fellow sank. His hat was floating around afterwards. They claim they dragged that place for bodies and never found any. That's a lot of baloney. Oh man, what they wouldn't do. I'll never forget it as long as I live. They tell you no one drowned that day. I know better. I saw it.

The papers claimed the sheriff was shot by an IWW. Well, there was a nurse at Providence Hospital where he was taken who told us it was impossible for him to have been shot from the boat. The bullet slanted down. We think he was so damn drunk—he was drunk all the time anyhow—that he shot himself pulling out his own gun. His deputy got shot, too, but he was shot in the back, which could not have been from the ship. His wife would show the clothes he was wearing that day. There was a hole in the jacket in the back, but no hole in the front. We wrote up the truth about these things and sent it to the newspapers, but they wouldn't print it.

One night the old hall was raided and everything carried into the middle of the street and burned. I was out of a job. I started to look for work in the saw mills. As soon as they found out who I was, I got fired. I went from one mill to another. Luckily, there was one old Jew who would hire me to load scrap iron. This was during the war, and he would hire Wobblies all the time. That was one job they couldn't get me fired from. Then one day the police came for me while I was at work and took me to see the mayor. He told me that some Russian boats had come into Seattle with money for us to make a revolution, and he wanted to know how much I had gotten. I had to laugh. I said I wish I had some of that money, cause I was broke. He says, "Mr. Peterson, it's time you made good in this town. You've been here quite a while now, and we've had nothing but trouble with you." I told him I was having trouble getting a job. "Well, you better quit them radical ideas you got," he says.

Eventually, I got a job working on the streetcars. I had a running feud with Paddy Ryan who was the cop on the beat. He got on my car every evening. Cops and priests could ride free. He'd come in and plump himself in the first seat. He wasn't supposed to take any seat if it was crowded, so when a lady come in with a little girl and packages, I made him get up. He looked daggers at me, but he didn't do anything. He knew darn well the passengers would be on my side. I must admit I would harass him any way I could, but he had it in for me. One day he got hold of the inspector of the line, telling him that I was a troublemaker. The inspector answered him, "Paddy, I'd rather have one man like Peterson on a streetcar than a dozen men like you." Boy, did that shake him up.

Another thing about that job was that I hadn't been on it for long when I was called into the superintendent's office. He said two policemen had told him I was a member of the IWW and that I shouldn't have a job. He wanted to see my card. I felt sure I was finished and showed it to him. He says, "I never saw a card like that before," but then he told me his own story. As a young man in Boston, he was already streetcarring, as he was now, and he had belonged to the Knights of Labor. He knew all about labor's problems. He says, "Here's your card. You stay on the job. I don't give a damn what they say." They still tried other ways to get me fired, but it never worked. About three years later, this old fellow retired and we got a new superintendent. I quit because I was also having family trouble. I had a crack at all kinds of jobs. I drove a team of mules on a road gang in Kentucky and beat my way on a river steamer in the same state.

One vulnerability the IWW had concerned membership. All we asked was if the guy was a worker. If the answer was yes, he got a card. In Everett, we had a guy who said he was a worker and we found out later he owned an apartment house. We got a committee and went to take up his card, but he wouldn't give it up. He was an old sourdough from Alaska who had made his money up there and knew the workman's side of things. He never came to meetings, but he wouldn't give up his card. He says, "I'm one of you," and he was. He helped out in every way he could, with money and everything else. That was a guy who should not have belonged, but who worked out fine. Usually those who didn't rate being members were destructive. A lot of them were Pinkertons. We could usually spot them, because they'd get up and start preaching violence in public or at meetings. They were put in our ranks to disrupt us. They still do that to labor and other groups.

I'm not an official member of the IWW anymore. I quit paying dues in 1976, but I've still got a card. I'm not good anymore for the organization. I'm out of a racket. But I don't approve of those AFL-CIO unions. They're organized like Heinz pickels—fifty-seven varieties in one industry. They can't get power that way. I'd like to live for another fifty years because I know things will change. For what, I do not know. Maybe they will kill all the working class and only use machinery. You don't even need brains anymore; you can use a computer. Through the years the Wobblies must have put out over a million red cards. How many have we got today? Maybe seven hundred. So we are not reaching the working class. They still have us killing each other on battlefields. Big money is still supreme. The big boys have many tricks up their sleeves and many ignorant workers are still sticking up for them, too many. One fellow gets a better job than another and thinks he's better, and so forth.

We sent an IWW delegate to Russia right after the revolution to see what it was like. He came back and said the revolution was right, but the wrong people were getting hold of it. That's what I fear will happen here. Something like that.

If people would get organized and get together, they could do things in a sensible way. We wouldn't have to use violence. We wouldn't have to use ammunition or weapons. The trouble is that people don't do that. I think they'll never do things in a sensible way.

Violet Miller

I first saw my husband Jack in a play put on at the Finnish Hall in Seattle. That was on New Year's Eve in 1923 when they opened that hall to the public. A lot of the Finnish people were loggers, and they had a close rapport with the IWW. The play was called *The Kangaroo Court* and Jack had two parts: the dying man and the stool pigeon. I went with my parents, and when it was over, my mother said: "That guy knows so much, you better watch it. He might really be a stool pigeon. I don't trust him."

Afterwards, at IWW entertainments, Jack would come up to me and ask for a dance. We got acquainted that way. My mother said: "Now you've met him. You know very well that the way he combs his hair isn't too good. He's kind of funny looking. I don't know." But we kept on going to the hall together—my father and I and my mother—and I kept dancing with Jack. I also went to some of the general meetings and to the meetings of the small industrial union. My first official date with Jack was for the May Day Picnic. From then on we saw each other often, and we got married on the sixth of September, 1923.

My folks had gotten involved in the IWW before they came to Seattle in 1922, when we were still living in the small town of Roslyn. There was an IWW delegate there who got my father into the organization. My parents weren't too active, but we read the *Union Record*, which was a very progressive newspaper. It had a columnist, Ruth Ridgeway, who gave me seven names of IWWs who had been sent to jail for their activities in California. I wrote to a man east of the mountains who had some kind of little machine shop, and I wrote to one of the prisoners in Leavenworth. When this second man got out of jail, he came to Roslyn and stayed with my folks. He must have been very young when he went in, because at the time he got his release he was barely twenty-one. Unfortunately, jail had had a bad influence on him. We used to have friendly card games, and he wouldn't be on the square. Then he would go downtown and gamble there, too. My folks were keeping him. He had no work and didn't seem to be looking. Finally, I went over to stay with my sister and he left. So all the

IWWs were not like Jack.

One thing I would like to say is that when people talk about the IWW now or in those days, they usually say "him," so you think there were only "he's" out there. Men certainly were in the majority, because women didn't work out of the home so much. But those that did were right there with the men and so were the wives. I was in one of those deals where you help out the men who are in jail and things like that. I remember Gurley Flynn coming to talk in our town. She was really good. She would fit in today for women's rights. She would talk about how women were discriminated against on the job, which they were and still are. So we did have our women fighters. I have a book at home which says that women are natural conservatives, which I think in a way almost seems true. But I look for a day when there will be more equality between men and women on the job and elsewhere. Then that conservatism will be lost. I believe we all have a right to work and earn our way. We are not going to have anything equal between the sexes until we have that. A woman can't live off a man and still be equal.

Let me say something else about that: I think we should do work that we like to do. If that happens, instead of a job being work, it is almost like play. Not every woman might like to be a housewife. She might be cut out for something else. I think a woman should have the right to do the kind of things she might like to do. My husband and I are senior citizens now. No one has to pay us to sing and no one has to pay us to do things. Even now we are helping to build a better world. We are fighting this discrimination against aging. We are both rebels and we will probably remain so as long as we are conscious. My husband is a great talker, but he doesn't sing. I do. So I would like you to remember this Joe Hill song:

There are women of many descriptions
In this queer world as everyone knows.
Some have beautiful mansions
And are wearing the finest of clothes.
There are blue-blooded queens and princesses
Who have charms made of diamonds and pearls.
But the only thoroughbred lady
Is the Rebel Girl.

> *I remember sitting on a bed next to him in the*
> *first months we met, listening to him tell me*
> *about his Pinkerton days when an officer of*
> *Anaconda Copper Company had offered him five*
> *thousand dollars to kill Frank Little.... I think I*
> *can date Hammett's belief that he was living in*
> *a corrupt society from Little's murder. In time,*
> *he came to the conclusion that nothing less than*
> *a revolution could wipe out the corruption.*
> —Lillian Hellman
> *Scoundrel Time*

HARD ROCK MINING

The Western Federation of Miners had been the principal force behind the creation of the IWW. Even after the WFM leadership, partly motivated by personal antagonisms and ambitions, took the union out of the IWW, the rank and file remained profoundly influenced by IWW ideals. Many miners carried two union cards, and in times of crisis, WFM locals often fused with the IWW or followed its leadership.

One of the sources of miners' fierce identification with the IWW stemmed from a Nevada organizing drive begun shortly after the founding convention. The campaign was led by Vincent St. John, and the local included many veterans of the recent WFM battles in Cripple Creek and Telluride. Before long the IWW had organized twenty thousand workers in Goldfield and neighboring Tonapah. The local included not only industrial workers and miners, but newsboys, croupiers, maids, dishwashers and prostitutes. Class lines became sharply drawn and shooting incidents became relatively common. In one of these incidents,

• *Frank Little.*

St. John was shot in both hands by a company agent, leaving his right hand permanently paralyzed.

The turning point in the ongoing struggle for economic dominance came in 1907 when business decided to bring in the AFL to take job control away from the IWW. This move was coupled with attempts to feed the growing rupture between the national WFM and the IWW and by a successful effort to have the federal government provide troops to maintain "law and order." No sooner had the troops arrived than employers felt free to cut wages and to insist on yellow dog contracts.[1] Perhaps the radical miners would have succumbed to the federal pressure and the economic counter-attack under any circumstance, but the anti-IWW activities of the AFL and the national WFM doomed their resistance. By 1908 power had slipped back to the bosses. All that remained was a legend that for a full year in a place called Goldfield the bosses had come to the workers to negotiate and that the terms agreed on had been enforced without written contracts or other paraphernalia of conventional unions. The spectre of Goldfield continued to haunt owners and inspire miners for another decade. Later the Goldfield experience was given forceful literary expression in John Dos Passos' *The Forty-Second Parallel*, the first volume of *USA*.[2]

Nearly every year of the IWW's existence brought some radical activity in mining, be it a coal strike in West Virginia (1912), a bauxite strike in Utah (1913), or an iron ore strike in the Mesabi (1916). By the spring of 1917, the IWW focus was on the copper mines of Arizona and Montana. As strikes and talk of strikes became widespread, the mine owners complained that the fledgling war effort was being crippled by an IWW that was certainly unpatriotic and probably treasonous. Without deigning to demonstrate their own patriotism by lowering profit margins or introducing long overdue safety measures, the copper interests mobilized local and national campaigns to drive the IWW from the mining camps.

Favored mechanisms for anti-union activity were Loyalty Leagues, ostensibly organized to support the war effort. One mission of the Leagues was to force "pro-Germans" from the workplace and even from a given geographic region. Any worker inclined to militant direct action was self-evidently anti-American and pro-German. Expulsions in most places involved relatively small numbers of workers and were held in check where trade union sentiment ran strong. But a hard-fought strike in Bisbee, Arizona, elicited a response unprecedented in scale or duration.

Sheriff Wheeler, working at the behest of Bisbee mine owners,

sealed off an entire county. No individual could leave or enter without Wheeler's permission and all civil liberties were suspended. This extraordinary plot was set in motion at dawn on July 12, 1917, when two thousand armed deputies raided the homes of all striking miners. Twelve hundred strikers were herded to a local baseball park, where they were informed they were going to be deported and that anyone who dared return would do so at the risk of his life. Later that day a train transported the miners to the middle of a New Mexican desert, where deaths were averted only by the intervention of Army officers who took the strikers to a military camp at Columbus, New Mexico.

Most of the deportees remained in the Columbus stockade for nearly three months, treated as if they were criminals rather than victims of a mass kidnapping. The legal remedies sought in the courts dragged on for years and the affair brought a change in the governorship of Arizona, but the immediate effect was that the back of the Arizona copper strike was broken. That autumn, as the national IWW leaders were being rounded up on federal indictments, the deportees had to arrange to remove their families from Bisbee to more congenial areas. Although the strikers had been forcibly transported across state lines and although the sheriff had disrupted interstate commerce by cutting off railroad, telephone, and telegraph communications, the Supreme Court eventually ruled the Bisbee deportations did not come under federal jurisdiction. One can easily imagine what the ruling would have been had the IWW sealed off a county and expelled the mine owners and non-strikers from their respective homes. Claims that the deportations were aimed at subversive elements proved to be fraudulent when a subsequent federal report showed that 62 of the deportees were veterans of the armed services, 205 owned Liberty bonds, 472 were registered for the draft and 520 owned property in Bisbee.

The intimidation of strikers was to be even more brutal in Butte, Montana, the other major locus of the copper strike. Butte had had a union tradition since the 1870s and was often a center of WFM radicalism. Chronic grievances regarding safety once more came to a head when a June fire in one of the mines caused 164 deaths. Fourteen thousand miners responded with a strike. Wobblies were involved from the onset, and soon federal troops were on the scene.

Also on the scene was the legendary Frank Little, who had been in numerous free speech fights and any number of shooting battles involving the WFM. A year earlier he had been yanked from a Michigan jail by vigilantes who beat him and left him unconscious with a noose around his neck. The undaunted Little had proceeded to new areas of confrontation, including the copper mines of Arizona. He arrived in Butte on crutches, having suffered a broken leg in a recent auto accident. Little had come to the conclusion that the employers and government would stop at nothing to destroy the IWW. Consequently, he believed the IWW had little to lose by emphasizing its revolutionary goals and proclaiming its opposition to World War I. As always, his presence emboldened the strikers and infuriated the owners. His sense of the political situation was to prove all too accurate.

On the morning of August 1, 1917, after Little had returned to the Finn Hotel following a speech at a rally held at the local baseball park, he was awakened by six masked men. The vigilantes beat him, then dragged his bound body behind their car on a rope. They drove to a railroad trestle, where he was castrated and hanged by the neck. On his chest was pinned a note reading: "First and Last Warning— 3-7-77. D-D-C-S-S-W." The numbers referred to the Montana specifications for a grave: 3 feet wide, 7 feet long, and 77 inches deep. The capital letters stood for the names of other strike leaders. One of the Ds seemed to be a direct warning to Bill Dunne, militant editor of the *Butte Bulletin*, and the C was directed toward local miner Tom Campbell, a radical opponent of the conservative WFM leadership.

Frank Little's funeral became a mass protest, with over twenty-five hundred miners in the processions and many thousands more lining the five-mile route to the cemetery. Poems and songs were composed to Little's memory, while demands for an investigation were raised in the liberal and radical press. But the killers were never apprehended, and the brutal murder had the desired chilling effect. Local strike leaders had to go about their activities with bodyguards, and the miners began to drift back to work. An attempt to revive the strike in 1918 was smothered in a wave of beatings, raids, jailings and fines. Just as in Bisbee, the copper bosses had won the day.

The reign of terror in mining had devastating psychological, political and economic impact. The following eyewitness accounts of the Bisbee deportations by Mike Foudy and Katie Pintek, neither of whom were Wobblies, express the sentiment of millions of Americans touched by the IWW's perspectives and horrified at how the organization was suppressed. The native-born Foudy, who later became a rancher, was only a child in 1917, but his view of the long term effect on Bisbee's social fabric echoes the comments of Irma Lombardi regarding Paterson after the defeat of the IWW. The foreign-born Pintek, whose speech remained heavily accented after more than six decades in Arizona, only refers to events in Bisbee, but her family had been actively involved in earlier radical struggles in the mining districts of Michigan.

Mike Foudy

When I was a child, my family lived in Gurry Gulch, Arizona. To get to the bathroom you had to go out on the porch first. I woke up on the morning of July 12, 1917, and had to go to the bathroom. I went out on the porch, and looking across the alleyway I could see a fellow with a big gun examining a padlock on a bachelor's quarters. There were a lot of single men in Bisbee in those days, and one of them had a cabin behind us. I ran back into the bedroom where I slept with my brother and pulled the blankets up over our heads. My dad had been on jury duty over in Tombstone, and I didn't know he had come home during the night. When he got up, he uncovered us and we all went on the porch. Men on horseback and on foot were carrying rifles. We saw them check every lock and door to see if anyone was inside. Men were herded out of their homes. A lot of them had no shirts or hats. You could see a mother send a child running down the street with their father's belongings. The gunmen would not allow the men enough time to get dressed and wouldn't let them go back. That afternoon a solicitor for groceries came by and he had a white band tied around his arm. That was a sign to the gunmen that he was okay. We learned that the men had been taken to the ballpark and were going to be herded into boxcars.

The next day, when we were at school, the teachers asked if our fathers had been driven out or not. I don't know what happened to those who said yes, because my father had not been taken. I don't know how active he was, but he was an electrician and belonged to a union. Electricity wasn't so popular in those days, so I don't imagine they had too many members. But he was definitely a union man. At that time he was working for the Cal-Arizona Mining Company. He never went back after that day.

My mother didn't let us kids leave the house, because she was afraid. They had lots of men all over town with guns, and they had men on all the roads. Some days later we went to Douglas, and on the way back we was stopped on the road by the gunmen. Everyone was stopped. Sometimes you were allowed back into town and sometimes you were not. There were also some people who decided to leave town and walk away on their own. I really

• *Mohawk Gold Mine, Goldfield Nevada.*

think they was better off than the men who stayed to work for the companies. At least those who left didn't die of miner's consumption, like a lot of the fellows who remained did.

Those who were taken out on boxcars were left in Columbus, New Mexico. There was no water, no accommodations, no nothing. They were just dumped in the desert like a bunch of animals. That was in the time of Pancho Villa, and there were a lot of army camps around the border. The commander there decided to feed the deportees. If it wasn't for him, those people would have been in even worse shape than they were and many would have died.

I was just a kid then, but the reason all this happened was that the companies didn't want a union. It was claimed that after the deportation Bisbee always paid fifty cents more a day than Butte, Montana, because Phelps Dodge wanted to keep the union out. If that was the plan, they were successful. There was no strong union again until the middle of the 1930s. Before that, we had the yellow dog contract and the company-run unions. There was no safety provisions. There was a headline once in a local paper that no miner had been killed in thirty days. You see, so many people were killed that that rated a headline. They drilled what they call "dry." There was no water in the drilling machine, and the dust went into the miner's lung and they ended up with miner's consumption. Finally there was a state law passed that they had to put in two pipelines—one for water and another for air. The water was squirted in there to make mud instead of dust. Then the miners could breathe better.

Whether people supported the IWW or not, most everyone thought the deportation, or "the drive," as they referred to it, was a disgrace. The companies had used their cronies as gunmen and most of those deported never came back. They relocated elsewhere. My family was Irish, and I don't think any of the deported Irish returned. Of course, there were a lot of Irish who were company-oriented. But how could you support driving men away from their families and homes? There was never many men around here after that. You see the buildings and stuff that they built. Before, those houses had been filled. Cheaper labor was brought in later on, but we never had the men like before the drive. For years after if anyone ran for public office, it was said they had been a gunman or they had not. That tag stayed with them. Whenever something happened to one of those ex-gunmen, an accident or something, people said it was a payback for what they had done. Everyone believes the deportation was the downfall of Bisbee.

Katie Pintek

I was born in what is now Yugoslavia, but then was part of Austria. I arrived in the United States on September 28, 1908. My husband had come from the same part of the country as me, but he had immigrated five years before. We met in Michigan through my uncle and were going to get married. I was kind of afraid, so we put it off until April of 1910. My husband was already sick from working in the mines. That's why we decided to move to Arizona, where the air was good. We thought he would get better, which he did not. But he lived another seven years and that's a long time. If we hadn't come to Arizona, he would never have lived that long.

In 1917 there was a strike being run by the IWW. Pay was good but prices were getting higher and higher. With the war starting, the miners thought they could get more pay. Okay, well, one morning we had our car out selling milk like we did then. We didn't have the house I have now. We lived in a corner house with three small rooms. We was carrying milk to some of our customers when there was a bunch of people coming towards us. I saw a man named Miller was bleeding. I said, "Mr. Miller, what is wrong? What's this all about? You're all naked, bleeding?" He says, "We don't know nothing ourselves." There was a boarding house up there, and they throw them out of their beds four o'clock in the morning. They throw them in this line and say, "Get."

It was just like lightning and thundering from the sky. A bunch of men came by us riding horses and carrying guns. They picked up some more people. I saw a little chubby man. He was all bleeding and there were kids with him, but they put him in that line. We were told the men were being taken to Warren Ball Park and that there was a train waiting for them to take them to New Mexico. They had twelve hundred or so men down there. The office is still there in a big building. The government's renting it now. That day they had their machine guns on the roof. They were bragging how they were going to shoot if anybody tried to stop them. They know no one had a chance.

Now they come back in the truck and take my husband. He was spitting blood that day. You know how the sick get when they are excited. We asked, "What is it?" They said, "You know." We said, "We don't know. We don't know." A paid scab threw the people on the truck. They didn't have shoes, ties or hats or nothing. I asked our renter who was with them, we had a rented house down there, "My God, don't be so hard on him. Don't you see how he feels?" He held the gun, you know, those long guns, and knocked it against the floor. "We haven't got time. Get ready." So that's all it was. No shoes. No ties. My husband knew the fellow in the truck. He says, "Oh listen, how many times I took you out in our jitney and gave you cushions for the road and now you throw me on this truck." Well, the fellow didn't answer nothing. They took my husband down there and throw him in the line.

I asked Hugh Thomas, a man I called Tom, a cripple who used to drive the car when my husband was sick, to take me to Dr. Folley. Tom would drive the jitney when there was bad weather. You see, there are three stages of TB. If you've just gotten the second or third one, Christ couldn't save you. Well we went to Bisbee to see if Dr. Folley had something to stop the blood. We went from one place to another. Everyplace we went we had to put on a white band, a white band around the arm. Otherwise, he couldn't go through the line. They would stop you like a criminal. I couldn't find the doctor, so I went to a green store to buy groceries for him to eat on the train. I was looking for my husband after the store, but he wasn't there. I couldn't find him.

What happened was that some fellow who knew him well said, "My God, what are you doing here. You belong at home, not in here." But before that time my husband said to one of the doctors there, "I'm not fit to be in this group of people. You know that." That doctor told him to get back into line. He was too excited to know what he was talking. Anyway, the doctor couldn't do nothing. That other fellow got the sheriff from Douglas, who said, "Mike, what are you doing there? I'll take you home." So he took him, and my husband was home and I didn't know it. I gave the groceries to another man. "We have things at home," I told him.

The way they hold those men there was worse than anything I ever saw in Europe. People were standing and crying. It was like an army had prisoners. If they saw someone about to run, they were going to shoot. Two did get killed that day. But that was early in the morning. One was a striker and one was a scab. No one knows exactly who shot first or what happened. Later, they asked my husband to collect money for the scab that was killed, and he wouldn't. "I'm not giving for that scab. If I give any flowers, it will be for the striker." They held that against him. Then they got mad because we had a scab living in our house and we told him to move. We told him that good people were forced into the street because of what had happened, but he could find a room. He was still working. They would have treated my husband meaner, but they knew he didn't work in the mines. They knew he had come to Arizona for his health.

They put those men into boxcars, like cattle they put them. They take them down to Columbus, New Mexico, without water, without anything. They kept them there in the desert for twenty-four hours without a drop of water. In *July*. You know what July means in Arizona? That's why everyone was excited. They didn't know who to get help from or what it was all about. What it was was that the company was fighting the strike. They just gathered the strikers up and hauled them away.

I deliver milk to other people that evening, late. My husband was home with two children. When I was coming back, scabs were watching me from their houses across the street. When they see me at the corner, they roll some paper together and say, "Toot-toot." My husband heard, but what could he do? We were fearful for a long time. There were men with guns on porches. They would say that if the company give them five dollars to kill some son-of-a-bitch, they would. That give me a chill. They would say these things when I walked by. What kind of America was that? To give someone five dollars and a gun and tell them to kill me.

Wheeler was the sheriff in those days. Whatever he said was law. My husband went over to see him that terrible day to ask

• *Armed deputy forcing IWWs on board train, Bisbee, 1917.*

for protection. The sheriff gave it to him, but by what right did he do that? Why did we need to have someone appoint protection for us? By what right did he come into our houses? I don't think we need that kind of law. I knew two men who came back from Columbus, Mike Cassuma and Phil Carribage. They told them, "You can't go to Bisbee or else you have only so many hours to get your act together and get out." They gave those men twenty-four hours.

Things stayed bad until Hunt got elected governor. Christ, never did Arizona have such a good man as Hunt. He was the best. When we got him back in office, things began to loosen up. There was an investigation of what had hapened. The company was put on trial. Some of the workers sued them, because they couldn't get work and about what had happened. The company had to give them pay. My husband was a witness.

They would say the IWW was not patriotic, that it was against the war. Let me say this. If anybody attacks America tomorrow, I, who am here now for seventy years, who claim this as my home, I would go cook for the defenders. I would do anything to protect my home. I have forgotten that other country, even though there are people there I love. But when they tell me to send my son to kill my father and my mother, who are not attacking us, I am damn sure against it. Is this right or wrong?

I don't know much about the IWW, but they didn't need many organizers. People wanted to join together. My husband had been in a union, a chauffeur's union. He said that the IWW sticks together. He said, "These are my people." Well, I know this. They will understand when you are all together—if they beat you, they got to beat me. That's the way.

ONE

ION   ONE LABEL   SIX MONTHS, 50 CH

PRICE 5C.   CHICAGO, ILL. SATURDAY JULY 28, 1917

THE BLOT ON "DEMOCRACY"

Thrilling Story of the Bisbee Deportation Told by Press Committee of the Exiled I. W. W. Miners.

Homes Broken Into, Men Robbed, Women Assaulted, Store Closed Down — Mob Law Rampant When Bisbee's Corporation Thugs Deport Union Men for Refusing to Scab.

STRIKE UNBROKEN — MINERS MORE DETERMINED TO WIN THAN E

DEPORTED BELGIANS—
AUTOCRACY

DEPORTED UNION MINERS—
DEMOCRACY

It's So Different in America!

I. W. W. Detention Camp, Columbus, N. M., July 21, 1917.—July 12, 1917, is the day that we will remember for a lifetime. The master class, beaten at their own game of law and order, lost no time in using other methods which suited them better. The mines of Bisbee were practically shut down; the mine owners of Wall street were losing thousands and thousands of dollars daily and hourly. Parts of the mines were caving in, but rather than grant the workers their modest and just demands they resorted to mob rule. The

lesson long to be remembered by all the working class, beaten and on their last legs, threw off the mask of 7 sumed their true character of murderous thugs. Sev beaten and many of the men have cut and bruised he a gunman and a fellow worker. The Fellow Worker worked at the Dean mine before the strike.

#1   #2   #3
Poo   King Chan   Ong Sik

*We respect the Industrial
Workers of the World as one
of the social and political
movements in modern times
that draws no color line.*
—W.E.B. DuBois
The Crisis, June 1919

CIVIL LIBERTIES FOR ALL

Wobblies were civil libertarians by conviction and by necessity. The harshness of everyday life had led them to conclude that personal liberties must be inseparable from the economic egalitarianism that would be created with the triumph of their one big union. In this sense the IWWs were a rare breed of working class idealists for whom civil liberties were basic components of universal human rights.

Necessity was a powerful, motivating force in the Wobbly espousal of civil liberties because the IWW could never hope to organize the unorganized without the full protection of the existing Bill of Rights. Like other trade union militants, their practice tested just how real were the guarantees of free assembly, free speech, and a free press. Wobblies also demanded that picketing, mass parading, boycotting and striking be given sanction as uncontestable citizens' rights. The specific legal issue in many IWW trials involved the supremacy of the national constitution over local ordinances and behavior which conflicted with the due process concept of American justice. In pursuing these judicial battles, the IWW was placing its faith not in a court system dominated by its opponents but in the determination of the general public to force the legal system to function democratically.

• *IWW organizers Chin Poo, Hing Chan, and Sik Sui Dang.*

Extending the civil rights of the working class took on the same kind of fervor and mass character in the heyday of the IWW that extending the civil rights of black Americans would take on after World War II.

If the IWW was like most of organized labor in fighting to secure the rights needed for organizing, it stood alone in its doctrine that rights enjoyed by any citizen must be shared by every working person without regard to their sex, skills, race, creed or national origins. The surest indication of the IWW's sincere commitment to this principle was its treatment of black workers. During the later part of the nineteenth century, individual leaders of the National Labor Union and the Knights of Labor had tried to create racially integrated unions; but at best they had been able to establish a handful of "colored" affiliates, separate from and unequal to the parent body. The rule in all unions created by the IWW was total racial integration. This was exceptionally courageous in an era when Jim Crow laws were being strengthened throughout the South, when the Ku Klux Klan still marched in presidential inauguration parades, and when most unions did not consider racism a labor issue. The IWW approach was spelled out in its usual forthright style in a leaflet addressed:

To Colored Workingmen and Women

If you are a wage worker, you are welcome in the IWW halls, no matter what your color. By this you may see that the IWW is not a white man's union, not a black man's union, not a red man's union, but a workingman's union. All of the working class in one big union.[1]

Prejudice against Asian workers ran as high or higher on the West Coast as prejudice elsewhere against blacks. Many workers believed there was a yellow menace that would take their jobs or depress their standard of living. Even prominent socialists like Jack London, whose writing was extremely popular among IWWs, voiced such bigotry, and total exclusion or rigid control of Asian immigration had been a constant demand of American trade unions. In a sharp departure from this view, the IWW welcomed Chinese, Japanese, Filipino and other Asian workers to its ranks, once more setting a new standard of solidarity for organized labor.

An even more dramatic racial breakthrough involved Hispanic workers. Instead of asking for the exclusion of Hispanic immigrants, IWW miners and marine workers raised the demand for an international wage scale to guarantee and upgrade every worker's standard of living. In the Southwest, the IWW mine and harvest unions had very high participation by Mexican immigrants. On the East Coast, the major Hispanic connection revolved around the Marine Transport Workers Union, where some locals had more than fifty percent Hispanic membership.

The IWW was extremely enthusiastic about recruiting new immigrants from Eastern and Southern Europe. Rather than being the "unorganizable mobocracy" the AFL said they were, many of these workers proved to have had considerable political experience in their native lands. Within community after community, the IWW was able to make common cause with the newest Americans. In the period after the Western Federation of Miners withdrew its affiliation and before the successful drives in the far West, the majority of IWW members were probably foreign born. As late as 1917, Chicago could boast of two foreign language halls but no English language hall. These meeting places were distinct from the formal national headquarters where the dominant language was always English.

The IWW commitment to women's rights can be characterized as "workerist" rather than feminist, concentrating on the exploitation of women on a class rather than a sexual basis. But even while lacking a sophisticated analysis of the cultural and economic consequences of sexism, the Wobblies were adamant about the principle that all female workers must have full membership and equal rights in the one big union. Only the garment worker unions being formed at approximately the same time had a similar outlook.

Despite the IWW's egalitarian perspective, absolute parity between the sexes was rarely achieved. Many male workers retained conventional views on sexual issues, and there were elements of paternalism in the overly protective attitude of many male Wobblies toward their female leaders. Workers soon discovered that women often could gain a more sympathetic hearing in influential genteel circles and in the popular press. They also learned that because of the bad publicity that might arise, government officials avoided prosecution of women if possible and police were often reluctant to attack female strikers or female orators. On a more practical plane, women organizers were not expected to "rough it" in quite the same manner their male counterparts did. Another indication of the special status of women were the auxiliaries modeled after Mother Jones' mop and bucket brigades. Militant as these groups were, no men took part in them, and there were no comparable suborganizations for men only. Males who wanted to support a strike simply worked with the IWW proper, even if the strikers were female.

The complex nature of male attitudes is exemplified in the thinking of Joe Hill. In an article written for the December 19th, 1914, issue of *Solidarity*, he stated that the predominantly male membership of the IWW in the West made it "a kind of one-legged, freakish animal of a union," whose social events were "kind of stale and unnatural on account of being too much of a 'buck' affair." Hill suggested all female organizers ought to be encouraged to work *exclusively* with women. His aim was not to segregate female IWWs, but to utilize their skills on a crucial front where males had failed. Nevertheless, it is doubtful he would have argued that Wobblies speaking a foreign language should be used exclusively to organize that foreign language group. Yet his personal admiration for female IWWs was unbounded. His enormously popular "The Rebel Girl" was dedicated to Elizabeth Gurley Flynn, and another, less well-known song was written for her son. From his death cell in Salt Lake City, Hill wrote to then ten-year old Katie Phar telling her how important it was that she continue to sing on behalf of the IWW, and his last letter on the day of his execution was to Flynn.

The IWW did take a position on one major issue of sexuality, reproductive rights. Pioneer birth control advocate Margaret Sanger reprinted the IWW preamble in the premier issue of her magazine *The Woman Rebel*, and one hundred thousand first edition copies of her *Family Limitations* were clandestinely produced by an IWW printer and distributed nationwide through IWW outlets and supporters. Female Wobblies such as Georgia Kotsch, Caroline Nelson, and Marie Equi were major disseminators of birth control information.[2]

The role of Dr. Marie Equi in IWW affairs is significant from another civil liberties aspect, because Equi was a flamboyant lesbian who wore man-tailored suits and openly lived with her lover for more than fifteen years.[3] She became a Wobbly after an IWW-led cannery strike in Portland involving women for whom she had been a physician. From that time on through to her arrest for anti-war oratory at the Portland IWW hall on June 27, 1918, Equi was a fierce supporter of IWW causes. A measure of her popularity among the rank and file was that she was chosen to be the Oregon Wobbly to spread Joe Hill's ashes to the wind, a ceremony that took place in every state of the union except Utah.[4] This acceptance of a lesbian in a leadership role by rugged Wobbly loggers is yet another indication that for them class solidarity had the highest priority. Perhaps not coincidentally, Equi was sentenced to three years in San Quentin for her anti-war views.

A related area in which the IWW was open to unconventional

sexual behavior was the acceptance of "free love" as an alternative to formal marriage. This acceptance was fostered in part by the tradition of common law marriage, by contact with Greenwich Village bohemians, and by the influence of anarchists.

The only IWW policy regarding women's rights that seems short-sighted in retrospect was its opposition or indifference to women's suffrage. This reflected the IWW's general coolness to electoral politics. From the IWW perspective, the suffrage movement involved militants in a system that the one big union, which already granted women full voting rights, would soon replace. Because of the non-authoritarian nature of the IWW structure, however, women such as Marie Equi could take part in suffrage struggles without jeopardizing their membership or reputation.

A final observation on the universalism of IWW solidarity is that a considerable number of Native Americans were members. Frank Little, one of the most beloved IWW leaders, was part Cherokee. Intensely proud of this heritage, he often teased other IWWs by saying he was the only genuine red and the only real American in the crowd. Not least among his services to the IWW was his role in forming the Agricultural Workers Organization and its job delegate system. No other Native American has ever attained the kind of influence within an American trade union that Frank Little enjoyed in the IWW.

Roger Baldwin, founder of the American Civil Liberties Union, was among the many intellectuals who developed an affinity for the Wobblies. Like others, Baldwin was attracted by the intense democratic vision of the IWW and then came to understand that many Wobblies were far more spiritual and philosophical than their appearances often suggested. Although Baldwin's brief membership sprang mainly from intellectual and class curiosity rather than personal need, his long-time support of the IWW was invaluable. With J. Edgar Hoover acting as the major field organizer of the federal assault on the IWW and Baldwin emerging as one of its steadfast defenders, the personalities and terms were set for civil liberties conflicts that would rage for another fifty years, involving other unions, other wars and other dissidents. Baldwin draws on that history to point out parallels between the pre-World War I Wobblies and the radical movements of the 1960s.

Art Shields, a journalist for the labor and Communist press for many years, recalls the last major free speech fight which took place even as the IWW was disintegrating. He then links the ideals expressed in that struggle with the IWW vision he had become familiar with in the Seattle general strike of 1919 and the Paterson silk strike of 1913.

Roger Baldwin

The IWW was involved in one of the greatest historic trials of free speech in the history of the United States. I refer to the 101 Wobblies tried in Chicago in 1918 for obstructing recruiting and enlistment for the armed forces. What was historic was that all the charges were based on speeches or materials that had been printed in the IWW press. There were no other charges. The crime supposedly committed was one of language, of condemning World War I in a way that was construed to discourage people from joining the army. This wasn't the only case to be sure. Almost a thousand people were tried during the war under the same Espionage Act. Never had so many Americans been prosecuted during one short time period for what they had said or printed. As far as the IWW was concerned, I have no doubts that the government hoped to destroy the organization with this prosecution.

Judge Landis, who tried the case, seemed to be very fair all the way through. His savage animus against the IWW was only evidenced when it came to the sentencing. He was playing to the gallery, I think. He felt he had to encourage the war and satisfy the government. I think the harsh sentences were due to the war hysteria. By the time the high courts got involved, Bill Haywood and a few others who were out on bail had left the country and gone to Russia. That was a very tragic thing for those left behind, because they had to pay the people who had guaranteed bail. The boys did a heroic job. They didn't pay it all back, but they did pay back a lot. Personally, I never could forgive Bill Haywood for that. When I finally saw him again in Moscow in 1927, we didn't discuss his defection. He went to the refuge offered to him because he just couldn't face a long term in jail.

It took us several years to free the Wobblies convicted in various trials. Quite a moral dilemma developed. At one point the government wanted them to apply for a pardon, which meant they accepted their convictions. Many of them refused to give even lip service to the idea that they had committed a crime. I told them I would write a letter that would not imply guilt. I wanted some kind of compromise to get them out. It created two factions and a deep moral wound. The IWWs were very moral people.

The organization received a second legal blow when the Palmer Raids took place. These were aimed mainly at alien radicals, largely those attracted to the new communist movement. I met with a group of about thirty IWWs who were deported. One of them was a Scotsman who became a very good friend of mine. He was deported simply for joining the IWW. Another deportee was an Englishman, one of the IWW poets. He was sent to London. There were Scandinavians and Russians in that group I talked with. I knew of between 150 and 170 who were deported. The rest of the IWW members I was acquainted with were one hundred percent American. By that I mean they were born and bred here. They were American to the bone and could not be

• *IWWs deported as result of the Palmer Raids.*

touched with laws aimed at aliens.

One of the Chicago defendants I came to know very well was Ralph Chaplin. After they were sent to prison, we staged a kind of children's crusade. We had the wives and the children of men convicted under the Espionage Act go to Washington, D.C., to lobby. There were many Oklahoma socialists who had taken up arms against the draft, there were the IWW boys, there were members of the Socialist Party, and so many others. We gathered about thirty women and twenty children and took them to the Capitol. Among this group was Ralph Chaplin's little boy, who was then ten. I used to go to Washington every week to work on the cases. Ralph's son kind of adopted me as a father. We stayed friends until his death only a few years ago.

When we got Ralph out of prison, I got to know him well, too. I visited him whenever I was in Chicago, often staying with him. He was a highly literate man, well read in the classical literature. He wrote a book about the IWW and was sixty when he published his last collection of poems. After leaving Chicago, he joined an organization on the Pacific Coast that tried to keep peace between labor and capital; and, finally, he joined the Roman Catholic Church. While he was in the IWW, Ralph wrote editorials, composed songs, and did art work.

Of course, he's best known for writing "Solidarity Forever." That song was begun in West Virginia in 1912 when Chaplin was doing volunteer publicity art work for striking miners. The first stanzas grew from killings around Cabin Creek and Paint Creek. The rest of the song was completed the following year when Chaplin worked with the unemployed.

I hate to use the word, but in a spiritual sense he really represented the finest of the IWW's aspirations and ideals. He was looking for salvation all his life. The IWW was one form of salvation and the Roman Catholic Church another.

I didn't know Bill Haywood until the Chicago trials. He already had a big reputation from when he was a leader in the Western Federation of Miners and had been falsely accused of murder. He was very decisive in his opinions, but quiet in expression and very gentlemanly in his manners. He liked nice people and good food, so he could be at home with the middle class. But he had the qualities of leadership. He was precise, positive, friendly. People could trust him. I had confidence in him from the beginning and had what might be called a very affectionate relationship, because he had a great understanding of what I was doing. He was an impressive man.

I first met Elizabeth Gurley Flynn at the time of the trials. She was a member of our civil liberties group but not very active, because she had her own organization, the Workers Defense League. She was very striking, what you would think of as a very pleasant Irish housewife. She was a little plump, very humorous, very smart, very wise, and very personable. One of my friends called her "200 pounds of horse-sense." She was very influential. She was a good civil libertarian until she joined the Communist Party, which I believe does not respect civil liberties. That's why we had to part company with her. But she was a personal friend. I visited her at home. I knew her son, her sister, her family. I was a great admirer of Elizabeth Gurley Flynn.

Vincent St. John didn't come to New York very often, so I didn't know him very well. When he did come, I would see him with Elizabeth Gurley Flynn, who was very fond of him. If there was a struggle of some kind within the IWW between St. John and Haywood, she was on St. John's side. I didn't know the issues, because I was not involved. St. John was quite the opposite of Haywood. He was a simple miner from the West. He was very quiet, but he liked to tell stories and there was a fire in him. When they put him in positions of leadership in strikes, he was unyielding. He was very representative of the IWW sense of resistance. Haywood had much more of the pie-in-the-sky rhetoric. He won audiences. I never heard St. John speak in public. I don't think he was much of a speaker, but he was the kind of man who would be very good in a tight spot.

Many of the IWWs were migratory workers. They called themselves "blanketstiffs" because they carried their own bedding. There's migratory labor now, like the Mexicans, but the old-fashioned migratory workers were different. These were fellows with nothing in the world but the clothes on their back, a blanket, a few toilet articles. We don't have that type anymore. The song book reflected their spirit better than anything else. I realized when I read IWW literature and heard the songs that they were governed by an ideal they could not possibly realize. They were revolutionary in spirit. They condemned the whole system of what they called "dog-eat-dog society," a system where everyone lived off everyone else, but mostly off the working class. The IWW boys had very sharp and biting satires on society. They said things pointedly, expressing their disdain for most contemporary values. They had a parody of "Onward Christian Soliders" that they used to attack militarism and religion.

The first IWW event I ever attended was a forum in St. Louis. I was most impressed. I learned of the high character of these fellows who led such good, austere lives and were interested in all kinds of education. In the winter, when they had no work in the country, they had forums and would hole up in libraries. At the St. Louis forum, I just marveled at how these working men could talk on such a high level about public issues. There must have been seventy-five to a hundred people present, mostly men. Later I also heard Ettor and Giovannitti speak at St. Louis at the City Club, a forum for business and professional men. I was struck by the capacity of these working men to talk to a thousand people on such a high plane about the freedom of organization, recognition of trade unions, and other public issues.

I joined the IWW after World War I at a time when I wanted to work with my hands. My friends were shocked that I should dare join the IWW. I was a thoroughgoing pacifist at that time. I had been in prison as a conscientious objector and I wanted to do civil liberties work. The labor movement of those days was heavily involved in a major civil liberties issue—the right to form unions. I decided to unclass myself temporarily and become a working man who could experience these struggles in several industries at first hand. I went from New York to Chicago, because I was familiar with the Middle West and wanted to work in the center of industry. I went to the IWW hall where I had had contacts during the Chicago trials. I asked them if it would be possible for a person of my background to join. They said, "Why,

• *Everett office with members in doorway, 1916.*

you would be most welcome, fellow worker." They had a big party. Bill Haywood, the general secretary, signed my card and initiated me. All the boys sang their songs and I joined in. I call them boys, but they were really middle-aged men. One of the things that surprised me was that I wasn't alone. There were maybe half a dozen college men, including a couple of Harvard boys, who joined for the same sort of reasons as mine. The IWW attracted idealists.

Having a union card was not a practical need at that time. it was more evidence of identity and good faith. It meant you were connected with something. Since I thought of getting into an industry which had AFL units, I applied for membership with them as well. I wanted to be neutral between the IWW and AFL. I had no trouble. I was taken to an assembly where there were about three hundred men being initiated at the same time. We occupied a good sized hall and went through rigamarole and formalities. It was quite different from the IWW, which was just a spontaneous expression of good fellowship. This was very ritualistic. I got the card, but nobody greeted me. I was just one of three hundred.

I think I had to show my AFL card two or three times in the course of four months. I only had to show the IWW card twice, but it was very important. I wanted to have the experience of bumming a ride on a freight. I took a train from Chicago to St. Louis, and I had to show the IWW card to get aboard. The trainmen would not accept you without one. They knew the IWWs were reliable and decent fellows who would always do what they were supposed to. They were not bums.

The AFL crowd regarded the IWW less as rivals than as upstarts, as people who cast a very bad light on labor unions. They thought the IWWs were a bunch of agitators and troublemakers. Samuel Gompers, the head of the AFL, was a very skillfull organizer. He wanted and got good public relations. He even had some slight radical ideas of his own, but he couldn't stand the IWW. They called him a "pie card artist," one of their phrases for people who want nothing but more to eat and don't give a damn about the rest of the working class. The IWW also called Gompers a "labor faker." Their language was very colorful. They had scorn for anyone they thought was a compromiser or an apologist for the big boys. My own view is that Gompers was a very canny leader who held his own organization together against all kinds of opposition and difficulty. I think he was a man of integrity.

People must also understand that the AFL was split into many different parts. A federation doesn't always have harmony between all its units. The individual unions could be quite separated and were dominated by the craft principle. The IWW was entirely different. It was a solid fraternity that never made distinctions between industries or jobs. They tried to get their officers to go back to the workshops or into the field after a brief term. They did not want people to hold union office as a permanent job. The AFL created a bureaucracy from the very beginning, while the IWW never had one and never dreamed of one.

The press and the business community viewed the IWW as a very interesting, but a very disturbing phenomenon. The dramatic tactics used by the IWW were very threatening. I don't think they ever engaged in violence. I can't think of a single member that was ever sent to jail for a violent act. If an IWW was freed or on appeal, there was never any violence. But they would do other things that meant business could not count on them at all. They would take jobs in large groups in an industry, and when they got dissatisfied, they all walked off the job together. There was nobody left to work. They did this in the timber industry and in the harvest fields very effectively. They had this sense of united action, of solidarity. They acted as a unit. The IWW was an amazing fraternity of very poorly organized working class men. They really had no center, no national office, no leadership. It ran on the voluntary instincts of people sticking together and using their power of quitting a job.

The IWW succeeded and the IWW failed. It succeeded in impressing a revolutionary element into American public opinion, a feeling that had been channeled before only in some religious movements. It also used collective techniques that were the forerunners of those used to greater success by the CIO. The IWW failed because it was not able to adapt to the changes in the industrial field and it split ideologically. But I think that any effective assertion of principle is important. The IWW contributed to the history of the rights of Americans to organize and to express revolutionary views without penalty. They demonstrated workers could stick together for a common purpose, although widely scattered. The kind of solidarity, fraternity, protest, and idealism represented by the IWW is always relevant. These are the mainsprings for social action. You can see parallels in the religious movements and in some of the unions. You found it in the student movement of the 1960s, with Martin Luther King's movement, with women involved with equal rights. They all, in some way, look for equality, justice, and fair treatment. The IWW was doing the same.

Public opinion is always fearful of the unorthodox. Anything unfamiliar is upsetting. When you challenge the value of steady work, reliability, and obligations to the boss, when you become defiant and fearless as the IWW was, people get scared. The Industrial Workers of the World represented a force that could not be dominated or regulated.

• *San Pedro police use water hose on demonstrators.*

Art Shields

The Free Speech Fight called in San Pedro in 1923 had two demands. The first was a trade union demand, hiring through the union hall; and the second was a political demand, repeal of the anti-syndicalist law. Under that law more than a hundred IWWs in California were serving sentences of one to fourteen years, which usually meant about three to four years in prison. I had taken a year off to do muscle work, to get a change of scenery. Well, I had quit my job and hitchhiked to San Pedro, where I found the harbor tied up tight. Every longshoreman and seaman was out, thirty-five hundred workers. The local press said ninety-nine ships were tied up in the harbor. The IWW held meetings on a hill overlooking the harbor. We named it Liberty Hill, and you could look down on the ships and get a sense of the power of the workers. Oh, those were singing meetings. There was more singing than speaking. They sang Joe Hill songs. They sang "The Internationale." The favorite was the British transport workers song, "Hold the Fort."

The San Pedro police were not idle. More than seven hundred people were eventually put in jail. A speaker would get up and start, and the cops would grab him. Another would jump up, and the cops would grab him. Still, they kept coming. It seemed endless, because almost everybody was ready to take part in the action. One young sailor, a very nimble fellow, got up to speak. He began, "Fellow workers, we're all in this together." At that moment a cop grabbed him. The sailor slipped free and ran. The cop started after him but was tripped. Another cop made a grab but missed. The sailor climbed a drain pipe of one storage shed and swung himself up on a roof. He went across to a gable. The cop was still after him, so the fellow leaped to another roof and from there to another shed and then back to the ground. The crowd cheered and we started to sing. There were more arrests and then an announcement that the next day there would be meetings all over town.

The word went out and there was a demonstration of about five thousand people, a lot of townspeople and many wives. The seamen were wanderers, but the longshoremen had wives. They serpentined through San Pedro. The cops were afraid. We wound round and round the street and got to the jailhouse, where there were about fifty IWWs. Someone in the jailhouse broke windows, and they began to sing a variation of a song that was composed in Chicago in 1917 or 1918. The song was written by Harrison George. The refrain ran like this: "In Chicago's darkest dungeon for the O.B.U./Remember you're outside for us." And the people inside came back with "And we're in here for you." It was very powerful stuff.

I was handling publicity for the strike. When I first came, they had another man who turned out to be a Los Angeles cop. Later he became a police captain, and we called him "Red Squad Heinz." He was suposed to be an authority on the IWWs and communists. Actually, Heinz was in there to be a stool pigeon and a provocateur. He made the mistake of trying to get a group of strikers to plant a bomb. They reported him to the leadership.

There were many donations for the San Pedro strikers from sympathizers. We got a lot of help from Japanese fishermen. They supplied the food kitchens with fresh fish. But strikers who lived in San Pedro had the rent to pay and the usual expenses. The biggest problem, of course, was police repression. An obvious person who could help us in that department was Upton Sinclair, who lived in nearby Pasadena. I called him and he said he was thinking of coming down to test out the right of free speech. He came and the whole town turned out. I was having lunch with him and wanted to get started before the crowd began to leave. He said, "I don't care about the crowd. This is a test of free speech. They'll hear about it later." When he finished his leisurely lunch, he and three men with him started for Liberty Hall.

The three men with him are worth describing. One was his brother-in-law, a big young fellow with a soft voice who really didn't know much but was a nice fellow. The second was named Hadman. He was a young devotee of Sinclair who had simply come to his house and gone to sleep on his porch and sort of got adopted. The third was a young millionaire named Prynce Hopkins, who spelled his name with a "y" and was very active in civil rights for years. So these three and Sinclair started for the hill with a bevy of reporters. The cops said the journalists could not go, but I and Rube Burrows, who worked with a little Scripps paper—it wasn't Scripps-Howard yet—pushed our way through. I guess the cops were taken aback, because they let us go. Anyway, Sinclair mounted a little soapbox which one of the others had carried. He began to recite: "Congress shall pass no law. . ." and a cop had him by the coat collar and yanked him down. Prynce

Hopkins jumped up and began to speak, and they yanked him down. The next two also started to read the First Amendment, the free speech and rights of assembly amendment, and they were arrested too. Then the cops made the mistake of taking Sinclair to an unknown place and holding him incommunicado. I raised a cry in the press that there was danger of foul play, that Upton Sinclair might not come out alive. As Sinclair was something of an international celebrity, this got headlines, which is what we wanted. His wife took it seriously and was scared to death. They let him go a few days later.

The San Pedro strike was called off after about five weeks. The IWW leaders felt the strike had served its purpose and they probably couldn't have held the crowds. But right to the end, the strike was solid. People went back to work together. The Wobblies said, "Transfer the strike to the job." That didn't mean too much in practice, but the experience left people feeling strengthened. There was some slight improvement in the conditions of the longshoremen, but the right to organize was not won until the next great upsurge in the 1930s under the leadership of Harry Bridges.

I was also active in the Seattle General Strike of 1919, which involved twenty-seven thousand shipyard workers in Seattle, another ten to fifteen thousand in Tacoma, and some more elsewhere. The strike was called by the AFL unions, but behind that was the fact that thousands of IWWs had gone to Seattle to get work in the booming shipyards created by World War I. There was ideology. The mood was favorable to action. My own union was the most left union in the metal trades. A lot of guys called for the emancipation of the working class. My foreman was an old-line craftsman and he would interrupt, "Brothers, this union is not for the emancipation of the working class; it's for the emancipation of the machinists." But the crowd paid little attention to that. The city stopped working. All the restaurants were closed except for the chains operated by the cooks and waiters unions. The diet of beef stew, coffee, and pie was a little monotonous; but non-union men got it for thirty-five cents, union members for twenty-five cents, and if you had no money, the meals were free.

The strike lasted five days. You can't keep a general strike going for long. But it was an extraordinary demonstration of solidarity. Unions established their own municipal functions. They had their own police. The union patrolmen with armbands were on all the streets and kept order. The government brought in a lot of troops and machine guns but there was nothing for them to do. One of the most dramatic movements for me was at the start of the strike. The Seattle *Times* was an anti-union newspaper. Its presses were

• *Elizabeth Gurley Flynn at Haledon, 1913.*

on the street floor behind a long glass window. The time for the strike was ten a.m. A friend of mine and I were looking through the glass, and at ten sharp, those presses rolled to a stop. What a demonstration of power! Unions had their own daily paper in Seattle for seven or so years, until the mid-1920s.

Back in 1913, when I was a cub reporter with a New York news agency connected with the Associated Press, I read John Reed's wonderful stories about the Paterson strike. I wasn't covering the strike, but I went over to take a look. I saw that the IWW had managed to organize workers that had never been organized before. They put the emphasis on immediate demands, but they held up a vision of a future when ordinary people would control the earth. Make no mistake—the immediate demands were stressed. It wasn't pie in the sky. The aim was something more now: shorter hours, leisure time, more pay, but with this eye on tomorrow. I heard that vision when Gurley Flynn spoke to some twenty thousand people at Haledon, not only strikers but people from nearby communities. She spoke from a small platform raised five or six feet above the earth. Her little podium was filled with flowers, and Elizabeth seemed like the finest flower of all. Underneath everything she said that day and everthing the IWW tried to do in the years that followed was this sense that the working class was going to take control of its own destiny.

THE GENERAL STRIKE IS THE KEY THAT FITS THE LOCK TO FREEDOM

> *I wavered in my allegiance to socialism,*
> *syndicalism (the IWWs) and anarchism. When*
> *I read Tolstoi, I was an anarchist. Ferrer with*
> *his schools, Kropotkin with his farming*
> *communes, the IWWs with their solidarity,*
> *their unions, these all appealed to me....*
> *The IWW had an immediate program for*
> *America, so I signed up with them.*
> —Dorothy Day
> *Long Loneliness*

COMRADE OR FELLOW WORKER?

The overthrow of the Russian Czar in February of 1917 was enthusiastically hailed by the IWW, and the October Revolution seemed nothing less than the dawn of a new age. A workers' state was no longer an abstract ideal, but living reality. Every militant worker wondered what the Russians had done right that everyone else had done wrong, and how much of what the Russians had done right was applicable to U.S. conditions. One of the reasons Bill Haywood and others cited for going into exile in the USSR was their belief that the IWW could play a major role in the new workers' International being created to serve as the engine of world revolution. While acknowledging they had much to learn from the victorious Bolsheviks, Wobblies assumed their own rich experience would be honored and their counsel seriously considered.

Revolutionary fervor among American workers peaked in 1919, the very year the new Communist movement in the United States was born. On the West Coast there was the Seattle General Strike, and on the East Coast thirty thousand workers in Lawrence shut

• *IWW picnic, Washington.*

down every mill in the city to win new concessions. In Toledo, Ohio, and Butte, Montana, striking workers jubilantly declared Workers', Sailors' and Soldiers' Soviets. The Boston Police strike of September was followed by a national steel strike of 365,000 led by William Z. Foster, an industrial unionist who had left the IWW to work within established unions and would soon become an important Communist. Wobblies were involved in all these events, but for the first time in fifteen years the IWW did not provide decisive leadership. Expectations about the coming revolution in the United States ran high, but rather than opening a new era of militancy the 1919 strike wave proved to be the last expression of the massive pre-war radical movement the IWW had done so much to mold.

As the 1920s commenced, the revolutionary baton slipped from the collapsing IWW to the organizations which would finally consolidate as the Communist Party USA (CPUSA). Given the volatility of dues-paying members, the exact number of IWWs who joined the CPUSA remains unknown. The Wobblies most attracted obviously were those who sought a more disciplined revolutionary organization that was willing to combine direct action with political action. Whether switching to the new movement or not, all Wobblies opposed U.S. intervention in the civil war in Russia and any aid to the counter-revolutionaries.

The original Bolshevik perspective for the American scene was that the IWW should be supported over the AFL in trade union matters, but that the IWW should also be urged to dissolve into the newly forming party. Many factors mitigated against this development. Even though the IWW was quite similar to the Bolsheviks in terms of its working class orientation and militancy, it was fiercely anti-authoritarian and rejected foreign domination of any domestic movement. A viable IWW role in the Soviet-dominated world movement was cut short when the official world policy declared for labor was to "bore from within" established trade unions, the very premise the IWW had rejected from its inception. To carry out such a directive would have meant dissolving all the hard won IWW unions into the despised AFL. The Moscow view that the same policy was simultaneously suitable for every nation and that this policy must be imposed on all parties belonging to the Third International was totally at odds with the decentralized and individualistic IWW perspective for social change. Americans in Moscow argued that approaches which had worked well in an underdeveloped Russia ruled by an all-powerful Czar were not always appropriate for the highly-industrialized United States with its functioning representative democracy, but their arguments were in vain. Wobblies began to feel that the successful Bolsheviks considered them second-class revolutionaries in need of guidance from their betters.

Quarrels betwen pro- and anti-communist factions began to dominate IWW gatherings and eventually became one of the most divisive elements in the schism of 1924. Similar debates raged in all working class organizations. The fallout from this ideological turmoil was that workers who might have gravitated to the IWW in previous years were left undecided between the two movements or opted for the Communists as the better vehicle for their hopes. Campaigns to free IWW prisoners and efforts to overturn criminal syndicalist laws were weakened, as many radicals strove to form a new party whose sympathizers were under nearly as much federal harassment as the Wobblies.

The major organizational difference between the IWW and what became the Communist Party was the concept of "democratic centralism," borrowed by the Communists from their Bolshevik mentors. Democratic centralism required obedience by all party members to centrally issued mandates that were to be arrived at through democratic consultations with the base units of the party. Historically, democratic centralism proved to be far more "centralist" than "democratic"; but even when operating as originally intended, democratic centralism involved a voluntary surrender of personal decision-making to the needs of the party as defined by the leadership. Party members were not allowed to disagree with party positions in public, and members had to accept tasks given by central authorities even if the work required severe geographic or familial dislocations. Trials of wayward members and their formal expulsion became notorious. These and other hierarchical practices of the new movement were predicated on the belief that workers required the leadership of professional cadre. Otherwise, at best, workers might achieve a trade union consciousness that did not automatically translate into socialism. Communists believed that leaving the fate of the revolutionary movement to untutored workers was so much wishful thinking.

In contrast to the Communist organizational method, the Wobblies lived by a kind of democratic decentralism in which every higher level of authority was rendered as powerless as possible. IWWs did not accept organizational limitations on individual freedoms. Members who disagreed with a particular policy simply didn't support it with their personal direct action and were free to use their own judgment on how much disagreement to air in public. The IWW halls and press were filled with criticism and debate which generally seemed to strengthen rather than weaken the morale of activist members. Wobblies were convinced that social movements that were not directly led and controlled by ordinary citizens were undesirable. The cultivation of elites and undemocratic habits within the revolutionary organization could only result in a change of power that did not meet their definition of a workers' revolution.

Discussion of how much cooperation would be possible between Communists and IWWs more or less ended with the schism of the mid-1920s. Those who remained in the IWW became increasingly hostile to the Communist Party. By the time of the Spanish Civil War, a decade later, the IWW would aid anarchist forces rather than the Communist-dominated International Brigades. Following World War II, the IWW would suport dissident movements led by workers in Soviet-bloc nations, with the most enthusiastic support for the Solidarity movement in Poland.

The shift in the thinking of Russian-born timberbeast George Hodin is typical of how most Wobblies moved from avid support of the Russian Revolution to distrust and then opposition. Hodin also grew increasingly disenchanted with the will of American workers to make revolutionary changes. After leaving the IWW, he worked with conventional trade unions and as a small-scale businessman involved in automobile salvage and construction projects.

Fania Steelink, also born in Czarist Russia, and Frank Cedervall, a major organizer of the last substantial IWW industrial union (Cleveland, 1934-1950),[1] represent the views of Wobblies who remained active after the 1930s. Steelink places her emphasis on rank and file workers rather than leaders and prefers action over theory, reflecting the IWW rejection of the need for professional revolutionaries steeped in ideology. Frank Cedervall hues to the worker-to-worker approach of the IWW that bypasses established government and party bureaucrats. He is incensed that workers throughout the world remain divided by religion, ethnicity and ideology.

George Hodin

I was born in Odessa in 1898 and I lived there until 1913. Among the first recollections I have is watching the fellows walking to Siberia in leg irons. Not too many were handcuffed. The Cossacks were riding in front and in back. People stood on the sidewalks like it was a parade. Odessa was a highly revolutionary center at that time. There were three universities there and all kinds of underground movements. The revolutionary feeling was not just limited to us Jews. I should also say that the Jews in Odessa never took a pogrom lightly. More Russians would get killed than Jews. I always used to carry a knife in case there was trouble. The police were the worst. They were very anti-Semitic.

My particular family wasn't too bad off, because my grandfather had served under Nicholas I for twenty-five years, which earned his family certain rights. This was important for Jews, because we then got the few rights the other Russians already had. That's how our family got to live anywhere it wanted. We were at a very low middle-class level. My father was a trader in real estate. Perhaps he would have gotten wealthier, but he drowned when I was just turned thirteen. I had a lot of trouble in school, getting kicked out all the time, so my family thought they would send me to my uncle in America. He was planning to come back to Russia in a few years. In the meantime, I could calm down and learn English. They sold my dad's library to raise money for the trip. And that's how I got to Seattle, Washington.

I only stayed with that uncle for a short time. My aunt turned out to be very religious and wanted me to go to synagogue, which I refused to do. My uncle said as long as I was in his house, I would do as he told me. So I walked out. I went to the Union of Russian Workers to find out where the jobs were. For the next four or five years, I just bummed around the country. I learned English. I worked in the logging camps. And I joined the IWW. At that time there were some Jews on the longshore, but the advent of a Jew in the logging camp or the saw mill was unknown. Even though I wasn't religious, I had a lot of fights because of being Jewish. I either knocked the hell out of them or had the hell knocked out

of me. Either way. The ones I hung around with the most were the Russians. Lots of times I ended up being an interpreter for a whole gang. In the IWW hall, at the IWW meeting, there was never any anti-Semitism in any shape or form whatsoever. It was only with some guy popping off on the job, an individual.

Among the people I knew, the struggle was mainly for bread and butter. Anyone who tells you otherwise doesn't know what he's talking about. First of all, the camps were dangerous. Even the simple jobs were dangerous. Take the whistle punk. What he did was put the cable around the log and hook the cable to the donkey that was to pull it to the landing. In Minnesota, where it was flat, they could use horses, but in the Northwest, where it was hilly, we had donkeys. Well, when that donkey was pulling the log it was essential to keep watching, because if the log got stuck in a stump the donkey would keep pulling until the cable snapped. If that happened, you could get your head cut off by the flying cable. So you gave a signal to the guy up in front to stop. It wasn't really a whistle, but we called the guy who did that a "whistle punk."

As far as the big names of the IWW were concerned, we knew of them, but we didn't meet them. We read about what was happening elsewhere in the *Industrial Worker*, which was a daily up through 1919. Of course, Haywood was known to everyone. He was legendary. One-eyed Billy. I never saw him personally. My mentor was James P. Thompson. In the vicinity where I was, he was the leading light, you might say the pilot light. He inspired me to quite a few things. He was the one who made me an organizer. The IWW didn't have a training school or anything. I just went with Thompson for a couple of weeks. He'd go into a camp, and I'd follow him later. He would talk to the fellows in the bunkhouse, and I'd listen and watch their reactions. After they went off, he'd ask me, "What do you think, Blackie?" And I'd tell him where I thought he was off. Later we would reverse the roles. I was more direct than he was. Thompson thought I was hitting too hard and ought to prepare the ground more. Maybe he was right, but I did it my own way.

I remember a medieval picture I'd seen somewhere. There were all these nobles who would sit at a banquet table and tear hunks of half-eaten meat and throw gnawed bones to the dogs. So that's what I told them we were—the dogs. I knew that when a man is starved or feels starved, he fights. Once you pass that point by winning some concessions, things change. We didn't have to use too much violence, but if something had to be done, you did it right on the job. You could run a spike through a log if you had to stop production. Or you might hire out a gang in a sawmill and then quit in the middle of the week and disorganize their work schedule. What I remember very clearly about those days was that when I was between jobs I never saw anyone drunk. No one drank around the jungle. There was coffee and mulligan and this or that. And discussions. A hell of a lot of talk. But no one got crocked.

That was the period in my life when I asked "Why?" about everything. Just like a kid. When you get up and see an injustice and there isn't a goddamn thing you can do about it, because you haven't got the power, you start to organize. It was easy for me to join the IWW because there was no regimentation. I was avid for information. There are a few people who have the ability to light up a fire in another human being. James Thompson was like that. Joe Hill, the Organizer, must have been like that too. I have the ability on a very, very small scale. I can sell ice to an Eskimo, but that's as far as I can go. I was hungry to know, and I would travel around to find things out and then spread the word. They called me Blackie because they considered me dark-skinned. That was because most of them up there were Scandinavians.

One time I decided to go down to San Francisco to hear Eugene Debs speak. It took me two weeks to get there from Seattle by the unknown largess of the railroad. They had marshalled all the police around the Hippodrome, because they thought there would be an awful lot of violence. They were very much mistaken. People came to listen. Debs was more like a labor preacher in his presentation. He was not a firebrand agitator. I was more fire-spitting than he was—that was all I knew. Debs could appeal to reason. He was a great man. As I see it now, I think he was too good to stand up in the harsh struggle for human rights. That time I went to hear him, I didn't have any money so I got a job as a coppersmith at the shipyard. It took them a day and a half to find out I didn't know anything about the job. That pay kept me for two weeks. In that time I heard the famous Emma Goldman speak. I liked her talk a lot, but I didn't think much of it was practical. I guess I didn't think too much of the female as a factor in the struggle.

As far as society was concerned, the worker was just merchandise that was plentiful on the market and had no organization to protect him. They put Debs in jail by using the war as an excuse. They railroaded him. My own sojourns in jail were only for thirty days, for "creating a nuisance" or something like that. I wouldn't put myself with the few who were actually persecuted for their activity. First of all, I wasn't that good. I was just a strong, husky kid revolting against anything he saw. A few days incarceration was no particular hardship. I looked at it as a lark.

What I say next is not very flattering to the American worker, but I found that they were easily satisfied. This was especially true with the native-born and the Norwegians. If one of them worked in a saw mill and had a chance to rent a small farm where he could marry and have a wife and kids, then he began to forget about the IWW. He dropped out because he didn't want to endanger that little security that poor farm provided. Most of the immigrants were different. They weren't scared of anything. They couldn't afford to be scared. They had more fervor and didn't resist the union the way the purely American bunch did. The Americans couldn't see beyond tomorrow. Until you found a way to rouse them, they were placid. Unless there was a big foreign element, the going was rough. That's an awful indictment, but that's what I experienced.

I don't want to make the foreigners sound better than we were. I feel we were ruled more by emotion than reason. Most of that came from ignorance and the harsh exploitation. None of us could make a living. All our strength and dignity as human beings was taken away in a struggle to eke out an existence. That's why the IWW had such a big appeal. We could associate together as people. Looking at that time from now, I can see that I was most interested in the immediate struggle. Once we got to the point where we had what was still a substandard but human way of life, we began to decline. We could take a shower, we had a bed to sleep in, we didn't have to pack a blanket. I remember a little Scotsman who was a defrocked minister of some sect. He said to me in the bunkhouse: "Blackie, you're just wasting your life trying to make a working stiff understand anything. The only time he will follow you is when his stomach is empty. The minute you fill his stomach, you can't talk nothing to him." I found that to be true. Once the crisis was over, the organization began to disintegrate. There was nothing to hold them together. The loggers already had got what they wanted.

The way I got out of the army had to do with the Russian exiles I knew. We had about five thousand Russians in Seattle. I say Russians, but they were a mixture. There were lots of Georgians and Uzbeks, for example. Until the war began, no more than ten percent were Jews. After that there was a trickle of deserters or draft dodgers and about half were Jewish. They would make it to Siberia and then to Japan and then over to Seattle. They were a very intelligent bunch. When I got called, they helped me get "rheumatic fever." They took my left knee and put hot pads on it. They they beat it with a stick and put croton oil on it which made it blister. When the doctor came, I told him what the disease was. He took my temperature and I remember this very clearly. I was lying in the bed and that old son of a bitch held up the thermometer with his right hand and slyly let his left hand touch my knee. Well, I let out a scream. If I hadn't done that, he would have known I was a fake. That's how I got out. I had the advice of experts. The average fellow I knew didn't want to got to war. In my opinion, Norman Thomas and the Socialist Party had more to do with the agitation against the war than the IWW. But one way or another, a lot of us didn't go.

I'd say I was a little different from some of the other fellows. When I was in town, I went with the Russian immigrants who debated all the time. I didn't say much. I just listened to their theories about this and that. There was wide disagreement between Lenin's understanding of capitalism and Trotsky's. When it came to anarchism, someone would bring up Bakunin. What I found was that most of those people were very intelligent, but what they had to say didn't apply much to the real life I found in the camps.

I nearly went back to Russia. There got to be about six thousand Russians in Seattle by 1918. Night after night they would dispute about the rigidity of the Bolsheviks as compared with Kerensky. The bulk of Russians coming through that had no special destination or relatives would go to these discussions at the Russian church. Another factor was a house set up by the Jewish community where there was free food for those who needed it. While they tried to place people by their professions or skills, the refugees were around to talk. There was a big division between the Zionists and the internationalists. Most of the youth were internationalist and would make wonderful members for the IWW. They had that frame of mind. Anyway, a bunch of us wanted to go back and fight in the civil war. The United States government kept you from going directly. From the West Coast you had to cross to Canada and from there you went to Japan and got a boat for Vladivostok. The cost was about $125. We drew lots to be on a list. Then whenever you came back from a job, you would throw into a common pot. A fellow would come from a logging job and toss in $5 or $10. As soon as we hit $125, the next name would go. There were only two people ahead of me when the Canadians shut the door, so I was stuck with being in the U.S., which I think was a good thing. If I had gone over there, I probably would not have lasted long.

Traveling in the jungles, I found that sitting around the fire the fellows would loosen up a lot, what they call "letting your hair down." You could learn all kinds of things. I don't think I have ever lived so freely as I did those years. Around the fire you didn't split up into groups. You sat in a bunch and listened or put in your two bits worth. There were no women. I never saw women on the road until the Great Depression. At that time I had a business with wrecked cars, and outside cities you would see whole families waiting for a ride west. I would fill up my cars with them. That's the only time I've seen the mass migration of women. There were occasional hitch-hikers of course. I'm talking about workers looking for a job.

When people found out I was Russian, they would ask me about the old country. I could tell them a little about Stalin. You see there were no banks then, so the revolutionaries would hold up post offices. The papers would report it as an armed robbery, but to us it was revolutionary. Stalin got to be known as a very dogmatic, very principled man. He had a terrific record of activities for the party and lots of popularity throughout Russia. When I left Russia on a Polish ship, the Polish sailors knew about him. I didn't hear about Trotsky until I was in America. But I was not attracted to the Communist Party at all. The rigidity and the authoritarianism of the party, the real setup became known to me when a teacher I had went to Russia. When she came back, late in 1918, she told us what was going on. The system had crystalized very early. There was no self-expression. As soon as Lenin and Trotsky got in, they set up the secret police. The rule that you would do anything for the party didn't set well with me. I was not attracted.

Fania Steelink

When I first came to the United States in 1907, I had already had wonderful revolutionary training in Russia and used to go to meetings about the IWW. I was working in the sweat shops in the garment industry, where I earned five dollars a week for twelve hours a day, six days a week. Of course the work was never steady. Most of these workers were girls. I had left Russia on account of conditions there. If you stood on the corner of a street to talk, you would be arrested. When I came here, it wasn't really much better. I had the freedom to talk, but I had to eat something too.

One thing that struck me about the IWW was the beautiful songs. It wasn't only Joe Hill. Plain ordinary people produced those songs. That should be a hope, because they came from the heart of the people. I remember, too, that even though I was very discouraged by conditions here, I began to read Emerson and Walt Whitman. I thought, "If America can produce people like this, I'm going to be an American."

I managed to get through World War I without many problems. Actually I can only think of two nasty incidents. One was in a cafeteria. They started to play the *Star Spangled Banner*, and everyone stood up. I just kept on eating and the manager came over and got very angry. He said, "What's that matter with you?" I said, "What's the matter with you? I paid for my meal and I'm sitting here eating. For me it's sacrilegious to get up wherever you are, whether you're in the toilet or anywhere else. I'm not going to do it." They let me alone, but they took my address. The next day men came to the little embroidery business I had. It happened that the woman who owned the building had the Bill of Rights on the wall. I said, "I'm not against the Bill of Rights. Here it is." So they forgot about it. The other incident was when the American Legion raided the IWW hall. The story was written up in the newspapers, and that very day our landlord came to say we had to move from his house. I objected because we had paid the rent. He couldn't do anything right away, but after the time was over, we were evicted.

All of us had been excited by the Bolshevik Revolution. There were meetings and meetings about what was going on. As a matter of fact, the meeting where I first met my husband was about Russia. They had put twelve professors against the wall and had shot them. These professors supposedly were with Kerensky, and they wanted to continue the war. I didn't believe they were guilty. I knew it was a bad beginning, which it was. I stood up and protested. Nicolaas got so mad that he wouldn't talk to me for a year. When we next met, it was at another meeting and someone was attacking Russia. I stood up and defended Russia. Nicolaas said, "How come you didn't do that the other time? We have lost one year." But I was against what they had done. I said they could have arrested those people, but there was no reason they should be shot. I knew it was a bad beginning.

In the past I rather objected to people who were trying to write about the IWW. They always looked at the big man. They never considered the thousands of ordinary people who did heroic things. Let me tell you about Mark Smith. He was a miner who knew Haywood and Ralph Chaplin personally. He got to working on defense issues, getting bail for people and things like that. He was paid eighteen dollars a week and was always traveling around and always broke. Finally he collapsed and came to live with us the last six months. He used to tell us wonderful things about the miners. And the brother-in-law of Haywood, he was a wonderful

• *Portland demonstrators support Lawrence strikers, Oregon, 1912.*

man too. He had no concept of danger, yet when he died, nobody was even at his funeral. There was a beautiful couple, Edith Cutler and Joe Tarasook. They lived in Chicago for thirty-five years and were always active. They had no children and when they died, they left thirty-five thousand to the IWW. I remember that no matter what happened in the IWW, Edith Cutler would forgive them and she would never stand for it being criticized. I used to ask her why she lived so frugally, and she said, "We still hope the young people will come, and they'll need the money."

The IWW had an element from the hobo jungles and an element from the cities. According to the people I met, the city people were more informed, fundamentally more revolutionary. They knew they wanted the abolition of wage slavery. That's how the preamble was written. But the people from the jungle, the ones I met, thought ham and eggs. They admitted it was a belly philosophy. There was another problem about different kinds of IWWs. During the depression, some ordinary people who never knew about "isms" got a good cooperative organized. Another group got together and made mattresses. These were ordinary people who could do things. But we had one fellow who could sit for hours and hours and quote Karl Marx from beginning to the end, but he couldn't *do* anything.

Frank Cedervall

From 1919 to 1931, I was an unattached radical. When I had graduated from grammar school, I had no inclination to go to high school. I wanted to learn a trade. But going down to the public square in Cleveland to listen to speakers gradually awakened an interest in books. I was particularly impressed by Dr. William Francis Barnard, a leading socialist lecturer. He took an interest in me and introduced me to the public library. The square I've been referring to had been dedicated to free speech in 1912 by Mayor Tarnell Johnson, who was quite a liberal. There was a stone platform available for anyone who wanted to speak, and there was a time limit so everyone could have an equal chance.

When the Great Depression broke in 1929, I was a plasterer. The contractor I worked for had some commitments, and I was able to work until the middle of 1930 when the whole thing collapsed. Most everyone was unemployed by that time. The next year Carl Keller came to Cleveland to make a talk on the public square. He had heard me speak and urged me to join the IWW. They were raising money for the miners in Harlan County, Kentucky. Jones and Hightar, the president and secretary of the Harlan branch of the United Mine Workers, were also members of the IWW. Two days after talking with Keller, I walked across the high level bridge up to Lockner House and joined the IWW. I went to Chicago shortly thereafter, where I soapboxed. In about two months we were able to get the General Defense Committee organized to the point where we could make a tour to agitate and raise money.

Looking back over the history of the IWW, I would say that we never fully recovered form World War I. One big problem for us was that the workers acquiesced to the war. They were so patriotic that they wouldn't listen to anyone who spoke against it. We must remember that World War I was based purely on economic motivations. It was not like World War II, which may have been more justified. The immediate result of World War I was that the IWW leaders were thrown in jail. Then with the success of the Russian Revolution, many Socialists and IWWs thought that must be the way to make a revolution. They placed their hopes in the new movement and ideology that began to form in 1919. Naturally, the American Communists wanted the IWW to be their tail, and when that didn't happen, they did their best to break us.

There had always been factionalism in the IWW. It was somewhat different from other organizations, because it wasn't over personal leadership so much. The major issue was whether we should be political as well as industrial. Among the founders of the IWW, Daniel DeLeon, who was also head of the Socialist Labor Party, was the leader of those who insisted we must fight with the ballot as well. The more anarchist element led the anti-political forces. There was a compromise for a time with each side modifying its views to some degree. There were four major divisions in the radical movement up through World War I: the anarchists, the Socialist Labor Party, the Socialist Party, and the IWW. With the advent of the Communist Party, things became dispersed. I lay the collapse of the Left in America to the influence of the so-called "Leninists."

For me, the IWW approach is still valid. If we look back in history we see that when the bourgeoisie began its rise to power, they appealed to the masses by speaking about brotherhood and liberty and other fine things. Diderot in his encyclopedia cried, "The world will not be free until the last king is strangled with the entrails of the last priest." Now that's a magnificent statement from that point of view. Personally, I prefer Thomas Paine's, "The world is my country, to do good my religion." The point is that feudalism was overturned by a political system known as capitalist or political democracy. We believe the time has come for that system to be replaced by industrial democracy.

Instead of voting where you live, you would vote where you work. It's better, for instance, in an educational institution to have the senior faculty, graduate students, teaching assistants and undergraduates determine who among their peers would be most suited to direct things rather than to submit to the governor of the state or a board of trustees. We would take this as the general pattern and through trial and error make it suitable to every situation.

If the human race is to survive, we must learn to work cooperatively. We need an AFL-CIO organized along the lines of one big union. Then the leadership could announce to the Russian workers that the American workers were going to stop producing armaments for war. They could speak directly to the Russian workers and avoid the bureaucrats altogether. The unions in each country could go to each others' plants to make inspections. If something like that doesn't happen, we face disaster. If we look around today, we see Irish killing each other in the name of Jesus Christ. We see Semites, Jews and Moslems and Christians spilling each other's guts in the name of territorial imperative. We see troops line the long border between China and Russia. I know that if Shakespeare had set the stage, he would have the ghost of Karl Marx crying out of the fog, "Workers of the world, unite!"

IWW Secretary: *Take some of those pamphlets with you to distribute aboard ship. They may bring results. Sow the seed, only go about it right. Don't get caught and fired. We got plenty out of work. What we need is men who can hold their jobs— and work for us at the same time.*
—Eugene O'Neill
The Hairy Ape

ON THE WATERFRONTS

The fulcrum of IWW influence in the maritime industry was the Maritime Transport Workers Union (MTWU). One of the strongest locals was in Philadelphia, where the IWW retained job control on the docks from 1913 to 1924. Other important maritime locals were established in Hoboken, Mobile, Baltimore, Galveston, New Orleans, and New York City. Shortly after the formation of the MTWU in 1913, a resolution urging affiliation with the IWW was passed by the Maritime Firemen, Oilers, and Water Tenders Union, which claimed twenty-five thousand members on the Atlantic and Gulf coasts. Even though this unity never materialized, the resolution is indicative of the strong impact IWW thinking was making along the nation's waterways. The action-crammed year of 1913 also saw MTWU organizers Frank Little, James P. Cannon and Leo Laukki active in the Great Lakes ports, where they recruited among the radical Finns working on the Duluth and Superior docks.

The success in Philadelphia was partly due to the racial policies of the IWW. Approximately half of the peak membership of four thousand was black, with the remainder composed mainly of

• *IWW seamen.*

Poles, Lithuanians, and Latin Americans from various nations. The major organizer was Ben Fletcher, the most important black leader to emerge in the IWW, and the local chairmanship was rotated monthly between blacks and non-blacks. The Philadelphia MTWU operated a closed shop and secured gains without either a written contract or a dues checkoff system. The local was also powerful enough to support allied initiatives in the area. These came to a peak in 1917 with successful strikes of local shoemakers, organizational work among sugar workers, creation of a federation of cooperatives and affiliation by a group of lumber handlers who broke away from the AFL.

Just as the welcome mat put out for blacks was crucial to the success on the Philadelphia docks, the full membership offered to Hispanics was key to organizing on the Atlantic run. Over half of all the firemen on that run were Spanish-speaking. Having been denied membership in the International Seaman's Union for years, large numbers of Hispanic seamen joined the newly formed MTWU in 1913 and 1914. By the time of World War I, a Spanish-speaking IWW local in Philadelphia was publishing a newsletter titled *Cultura Obrera* and the New York MTWU branch had nearly five thousand Spanish-speaking members. These Hispanic IWWs carried the Wobbly message into the ports of Central and South America, where fraternal groups or actual MTWU branches were formed in dozens of cities. Other seagoing Wobblies initiated similar branches in European, Australian and New Zealand ports. A measure of IWW power at sea was that one of the duties of the MTWU secretary in Boston was to prepare crews' menus for all vessels on the Atlantic run. These menus carried an IWW seal and were posted on mess hall bulletin boards. Cooks and captains who failed to abide by them could expect retaliatory direct action.

Some ten years after the IWW triumph in Lawrence had made the unionization of the textile industry a real possibility, the IWW had reached a comparable moment in its maritime work. The MTWU had grown to be a sizeable minority presenting a distinctive vision of a new kind of unionism. Referring to the 1923-1924 period, the official history of the IWW states that after a certain point, a new union "must forge ahead to replace the union it criticizes, or its adherents lose hope and drop out. The MTWU could not cross the gap; it was left once more a small minority championing the cause of direct action and industrial unions."[1] Thwarting the MTWU's ambitions were continued government persecutions and disputes with the new, untested IWW leaders over issues involving initiation fees, dues, and centralization. The Philadelphia local concluded that the national organization had gone on a bizarre ideological binge that was destructive to practical on-the-job organizing. The local withdrew its affiliation and eventually became part of the conventional trade union movement. Similar defections by those most concerned with job control took place in other areas of IWW strength.

While the IWW never recovered the influence it had exerted in the maritime industry between 1913 and 1924, it did not disappear from the scene. Specific ships remained under IWW control, and in various ports groups of longshoremen carried two union cards, giving the IWW a shadow existence as an alternative industrial union in waiting. When captains or owners were not agreeable to IWW demands, entire crews might be pulled from a ship just as it was about to sail. In 1929 a MTWU unit was established in Stettin, Germany, where it took part in anti-Hitler work, and as late as 1936 the IWW had the power to stop the *S.S. San Jose* from leaving the port of Philadelphia with munitions for the Spanish fascists. At various times and places in the 1930s and 1940s, the IWW would rise up in unsuccessful bids for local power. The tenacity of individual Wobblies was remarkable, and their tradition of direct action left a permanent imprint on American waterfronts.

The IWW record in the maritime industry has largely been ignored. This neglect is partly due to the central role played by black and Hispanic workers, groups whose role in the American labor movement has never been adequately recorded. Six months of leafletting and pursuing personal contacts on the Philadelphia

• *IWW longshoremen, Philadelphia.*

docks were needed to locate even one of the thousands of black longshoremen who had belonged to the IWW. James Fair, the individual found through this process, proved to be an important source. In addition to being the only person in this book who had to join the IWW in order to work, Fair offers a firsthand account of how the local functioned on a day-to-day basis and of how IWW longshoremen in Philadelphia responded to World War I. He became an IWW at a time when the local was being challenged on piers where it held sway, temporarily halting effective expansion to new areas. Fair's assertion that the IWW did not interfere with the movement of war goods is significant in that the Philadelphia docks were one place the alleged IWW conspiracy against the war could have had material consequences.

Swiss-born Walter Nef, one of the organizers Fair refers to, happened to be one of the few IWW leaders who supported intervention on behalf of the Allies. Although there was not a single anti-war incident on the Philadelphia docks, Nef was found guilty in the Chicago sedition trial. He was sentenced to twenty years in Leavenworth and fined twenty thousand dollars. Ben Fletcher received a ten-year sentence and was fined thirty thousand dollars.

A description of the IWW agitation among seamen during the period between the two world wars is provided by Fred Hansen. He recalls how the IWW sense of humor was manifested among mariners, but states that singing songs while at sea was not common. His recounting of specific grievances suggests the struggles on individual ships were much like those at many lumber camps. Relatively small groups of workers were pit against lower level managers representing absentee owners who had negotiated lossproof contracts with the federal government.

James Fair

Conditions on our farm in the South were just bad. My parents heard that in Pennsylvania, well, so to speak, you could rake up money from the street. We decided to move North. Soon as I arrived, I went out and got a job where I got twenty-five cents an hour. I had to do sweeping and cleaning, because that's all I knew how to do other than plowing. Later, I heard about a job on the waterfront. I heard about people belonging to a union called the Industrial Workers of the World. I went down and got some information and joined. That was 1917, the beginning of my union life. At that time, there was no such thing as the AF of L on the riverfront of this port. Didn't know what it was. We became affiliated with them much later, and then the CIO came in.

Those days two men would work a hand truck with two iron wheels. Our freight was things like flour, corn meal, grits. We'd take it over rough floors to the side of the ship to be loaded. We worked ten hours with an hour for lunch. The wage was about eighty-five cents an hour. Our problem was that people were getting hurt. We had no medical or safety rules or anything like that. The first accident I incurred was on Christmas Eve, 1919. I had worked up from the docks and was aboard a ship. We had what they call a turn hole. You're on the deck and have to work with a machine. I got caught in the turn. Its head caught my trousers and pulled me around. When they stopped the machine, my head was down and my legs were up in the air. I sustained a strained left knee. They carried me to the hospital, and I laid there in the hospital practically all afternoon before they even examined me. Since I didn't have anything broken, they sent me home. When I recovered enough to go back to work, I found I had no job.

The IWW tried to change those conditions, but it wasn't favored by most workers and companies didn't like it at all. I learned that the companies considered it a subversive organization, but we kept fighting and fighting. Striking was unlawful then; when we were on strike, people were transported from different parts of the country to break it. Every time we had a strike, they'd transport those men in vans with police escorts right from the starting points to the job. Strikers would have as much chance before a strikebreaker as a rabbit would have before a gunner. In nineteen and twenty-two, the IWW was out on strike all the month of September. We tried to do something at lunchtime, but the companies would feed the strikebreakers right on the docks. They won out. We had one stevedoring company come here and work right on Pier 78 which is in operation now. They helped to break the strike. This was something that I experienced.

The IWW was for the laboring man, not just black or white. That's why it was so opposed by the capitalists. I'm not a radical, not by any means. I do believe in moderation. I also believe in getting the most for my labor. I don't believe in getting something for nothing. I think labor is entitled to a fair turn, and that's what the IWW, in my eyes, stood for. But without a certain amount of radicalism, we wouldn't have had decent homes to live in. Now, this thing of working ten or fifteen minutes past the hour and not getting paid for it—they didn't stand for that. We finally got that in a contract years later, but there was a time when the companies cheated us on that.

Everyone got along fairly good working on the docks of Philadelphia. Now, when we left the job, that was different. But when we worked, we worked on the decks together, we worked on the wharves together, and we worked in the hole together. Yes, we were given the roughest jobs, of course. Because more than one time, if a white came along, I didn't have no job. My experience involved whites beginning from my advance from the truck to working on the deck. Maybe they took a liking to how I worked. If they told me something, I did it and I did it with speed. I wanted to advance. That was the way I got away from this hard labor, this worrisome work on the docks. It was rough. Nowadays a lot of automation has cut down the number of jobs, but I can appreciate the changes. Despite the things being as bad as they are, what longshoremen do today is not as back breaking as it was.

In those days, we didn't have a checkoff system. We wore buttons with a different color for each month, and it was marked with the name of the month. Men could be working who were far behind in their dues and the IWW might have to call a job action because the boss would not knock those men off. It was similar to a strike. The only time I remember a formal strike would be later, after we had contracts. There was no such thing as a picket line, because unions didn't have that right. We didn't have news media like today. Word just got around: we weren't working. I don't know much about what it was like before the IWW, because when I first came to the docks, the IWW was already there. They were the only thing on the riverfront to represent the worker.

We had some good leaders. Ben Fletcher was a Negro—we say "black" now—and we had another guy whose first name I don't remember, but his last name was Nef, and he was white. I don't remember his nationality, but he was a very dedicated union man. Both of them were. For as long as the IWW existed, our meetings were at 121 Catherine Street. They would call the meeting to order and read the minutes. Then we'd talk about whatever was on the agenda: working conditions and what-not were discussed. I think it was very democratic.

As far as blacks were concerned, things were rough. To my knowing, the IWW was the only union, at that time, accepting black workers freely. They advocated just one thing—solidarity. Ben Fletcher would tell us we had to live together and work

• *IWW organizer Ben Fletcher holding child.*

together. His pet words were: "All for one and one for all." Solidarity was the main thing. That sank in with a lot of us. It paid off, and it's paying off today. You see, the IWW was something for the working man. It didn't make any difference who you was, what kind of work you did. They wanted to organize *all* the working people.

Fletcher was not only just in Philadelphia. He was a national organizer. Some of us were very hurt when he was arrested. We knew what he was doing was something for us to earn a livelihood, to support ourselves and our families. It was just like, well, I would say it was something like Martin Luther King, but turned to organized labor and improving our standards of life. I don't think how the IWW felt about the war had anything to do with what happened. As far as I know of, the union, the IWW, supported the war. We longshoremen, a good many of us, would extend our hours without any hesitation. I was on ships myself in the Philadelphia navy yard at that time. We would be working, and they would ask us to work through, working at nights, for instance. They'd say the ship has got to go. Some would agree to work until seven. If we weren't finished, the order would come down to work until the job was done. Naturally, we would have some who would rebel. Some wanted to get something to eat and would get food off the ship. The companies began to station guards and marines so that no one could leave the ship. We'd have to stay until the ship was finished. That was because a war was going on. There were men overseas fighting for you, giving their lives. You couldn't refuse to supply them with food and arms and what-not. What I'm saying is not a fairy tale. I experienced it myself. In all walks of life, we find some people going to the extreme; but on the whole, I think the IWW promoted fairness. They said if you were hired, you should work. They didn't say break your neck, but they advocated work.

The charges against Fletcher and Nef were trumped up just to get rid of them. Since it wasn't local, they didn't go to a city or state jail, but to a federal prison. With them gone, activities gradually ceased here in Philadelphia. The IWW wasn't effective anymore. We had several other organizers come along to do what they could do, but the odds were against us. I remember seeing Fletcher and Nef going off to prison. Being locked up affected their natural health a lot. I saw them after they came out, and they were very thin. How long they lasted after that, I just don't know.

Fred Hansen

When I joined the IWW in 1922, I didn't know too much about the revolutionary movement. I was just a rebel and I knew that wages had been cut the year before and that conditions were lousy. The seamen had no organization and were subjected to all kinds of abuse from the officers, even though the officers had had their pay cut too. For a time, an individual ship's crew would act on its own to remedy whatever condition they could—overtime, lousy food, and so forth. These actions continued throughout 1922 and into 1923 when the IWW called for a strike. The strike lasted only three weeks. Although it was not complete, there was sufficient interruption to compel the owners to give concessions. The United States Shipping Board agreed to increase wages from $55.00 to $62.50 for able seamen, with raises for other ratings too.

Conditions became a little better, but the owners got busy finding subterfuges for getting around them. For example, there was no pay for overtime. Most of the offshore ships were actually owned by the United States government. The various shipping companies just operated them on a bare boat charter. In other words, the company supplied the fuel, food, and other things, and the government supplied the ship. The men shipped out of the United States government office called the Shipping Board. This enabled the owners to use the blacklist very efficiently, because if you were blacklisted in one port, all the offices would soon get the information.

We often resorted to job actions on individual ships because communication between seamen was almost nil. A general strike at that particular time was almost impossible. You didn't know what the hell was going on anywhere unless you got in port and somebody told you. If you was out to sea for two or three months, you never heard about what went on. So we used job actions on ships or against lines. The Bow Line had a bunch of ships running out of New York to Puerto Rico. There were actions so that sometimes the ships would sail on schedule and the next trip the ship would be tied up. There was no certain pattern that the ship owners could follow. That was a privately owned line, not a government outfit.

Most of the ships had these straw mattresses. They wouldn't always renew them after the trip, so you'd be sleeping on a straw mattress that a guy got drunk on and might have urinated on and done a good many other things. Insofar as linen was concerned, they gave you a sheet, pillow cases, and so forth, but you had to do your own washing. If the ship was out for six to eight months, which was normal in those days, you had a problem. The food was the lowest grade on the ship. Most lines had a two-pot system—the officers got one pot and the crew the other. The food was made differently, and there was quite a variation in quality and quantity. It was standard for the cook to tell a seaman, "There ain't no more." Some ships had four- or five-pot systems. The Captain would eat one meal and at the same table the Chief Engineer and Chief Mate would eat different food, and this would be different from the other officers eating in a different room on down to the crew, which got the worst. Then they had what they called "field days." Under the law, the members of the engine room could only work eight hours in the engine room, so the ship owners had them work two to five more hours on deck, repairing steam lines and winches and doing other work without overtime pay. They would say, "We'll give you time off in some other port," but before you got that time you was fired or quit.

When we had to have meetings we'd go back to the fantail at the stern of the ship to get away from the officers. Sometimes there'd be a stool pigeon who'd go and rat, but most of the time we had no problems. On the old type ships, the quarters of the crew was always back aft with midships and upforward exclusively for the licensed officers, so we had means of getting away from them. What we could do depended on how many members we had on a ship. We always tried to be congenial with the non-members. The extent of your popularity was more or less the gauge of how much response you would get to a proposal. Most of the guys feared being blacklisted. There were twenty thousand men on the blacklist. Not all were on for union activities. A lot were on for being drunks or missing a ship in a foreign port or not performing duties. Still, many were on for being in the union.

Some ships were pretty solidly IWW. On the Sinclair Line we had a ship that was almost one hundred percent for several years. The captain tolerated the situation—he knew everybody was IWW—because they was all such *good* seamen. They knew their job and there was never trouble. That was in the last part of the 1920s.

One problem we had organizing was that a lot of ships would

Join The

Marine Transport Workers Industrial Union No. 510

tie up after a single trip and hire a new crew when they were ready to go. Coastal ships picked up crews anywhere they could. It was hard to organize them, especially in the Carolinas, Georgia, and Florida, because most of them was farm boys and they was not really interested in a job in the maritime industry. As the 1920s started to fade away, the job actions became less and less and the organization fell off. We also had to compete with corrupt and reactionary unions. Anytime we walked off a ship, the International Seaman's Union would have a crew there. The struggle was kind of hard until the early 1930s. In 1934 we had the strike in the Gulf that lasted for eleven days in May, and later on the West Coast longshoremen and sailors walked out in a strike that was very big and violent.

One thing about the IWW seamen was that we didn't sing much. Seamen were a different breed of people. Ashore we'd mingle with people and hoot and holler, but on the ships you never heard singing. They might be whistling or mumbling or humming or something like that, but I never heard anyone singing.

We had quite a sense of humor. An incident that took place in 1931 is typical of that. We were conducting open forums in the Marine Transport Workers Hall close to South Street on Quincy Slip in New York City. We were not very successful in attracting people. A little actor among us, Harry Engels, said he had an idea about how to get a crowd. He was a very dignified looking individual and he got another fellow to help him out in his scheme. Engels got dressed up in a cutaway coat and had his friend dress as a valet. Right across the hall was the Seaman's Church Institute. When the seamen in there saw Engels and his valet standing outside the hall, they asked who the hell he was. We had a few of our stooges tell them it was Mr. Ward of the Ward Steamship Company. This company had two passenger ships running down to Cuba, plus a couple of freighters. The guys wanted to know what Ward wanted. Our stooges replied that he had come down to the waterfront to refute the charges the IWW was making about the lousy food and working conditions on the Ward Line ships. Everyone got stirred up and when "Ward" went into the hall, a long line of seamen followed him up those three flights of stairs like he was the Pied Piper. We usually were lucky to get a dozen, but that day the hall was full.

Jack Shannon was up front as the speaker. He talked about the food and other things regarding the Ward Line. Harry Engels rose up and said, "That's a damned lie! That's an outright lie!" He pulled out the first-class passenger menu. They had French names for various dishes, and he stated, "This is what I feed on my ships!" All the seamen in the crowd started grinding their teeth because they'd never heard of the stuff and, of course, they never got it. After Engels sat down, Jack Shannon said Ward's claims were not true, but the actor got back up and insisted that was the menu the crew was getting. Things began to boil and one of the seamen, not one of our members, but someone in the crowd, said, "Mr. Chairman, is there a motion to throw that son-of-a-bitch out the window?" We began to get worried there might be some real violence. We subdued things and concluded the meeting. When "Ward" was walking down the stairs, one guy went over to him and said, "I agree with you one hundred percent that these reds up here are telling lies about your steamship company. I know it isn't so." Our actor replied, "You're a good one hundred percent American boy. You come down to my office tomorrow, and I'll see to it that you get a job." Engels kept on acting even after he went to eat in a restaurant, but that's not the real story. The story is that the next day I got a telephone call from a guy who shouted, "I want to tell you IWWs that you're a bunch of goddamn fakers and liars. I went down to the offices and I found out there is no such thing as a Mr. Ward. The Ward Lines don't have a Mr. Ward. So you're all liars and fakers." I replied, "Yeah, and you're a scabby scum trying to get into the good graces of the boss."

When I first joined the IWW, I thought you had to be a union man to get a job, which, of course, was not true. But I had more or less a rebel in me. I resented being manipulated by people. Every place that I worked was casual jobs and people pushed you around. Even washing dishes, someone was always on top of you telling you you ain't doing this right or you ain't doing that right. So I was ripe for the IWW. I didn't know about the revolutionary part at first, but as soon as I got in the organization, I started reading an awful lot—not only IWW literature, but the communist literature, the anarchist literature, anybody's literature. I'm willing to read. I may not agree with the literature, but I'll read it. The only way you can know about anybody is to read about them. You can't argue effectively unless you know what they stand for and what their purpose is.

The IWW affected my life in a lot of ways. Naturally I was blacklisted or blackballed from a lot of companies. They used the doctor a lot to disguise their policy. He'd find something wrong so things didn't come to a confrontation. But I took a certain satisfaction in the fact that I was doing something about a deplorable situation. In the early 1930s, we learned from government hearings that the West Lashaway Line had a subsidy of over $300,000 for carrying one sack of mail to Africa. In those days, for that kind of money, you could have made five trips to Africa empty and still paid all your costs. So the shipowners always were making money.

> *Whether the IWW increases in power
> or is crushed out of existence, the
> spirit that animates it is the spirit that
> must animate the labor movement if it
> is to have a revolutionary function.*
> —Hellen Keller
> *The Call*, February 3, 1918

CONTINUED REPRESSION AND DECLINE

The criminal syndicalist and sedition laws passed by thirty-five states after America's entry into World War I aimed to wipe out local IWW bases and jail any leaders the federal net had missed. Thousands of IWWs were held under these statutes, effectively disrupting organizational drives and legal defense of federal prisoners. The laws were drafted in such a manner that conviction was possible for conspiracy to commit criminal acts even if no criminal acts were proven or committed. Establishing that any given individual was a Wobbly activist or held some IWW office was usually considered sufficient evidence that the individual was part of a criminal conspiracy.

War hysteria played a predictable role in easing passage of the anti-syndicalist legislation, but there was a popular perception that the IWW was indeed a violence-prone organization. Although largely based on inaccurate and sensationalistic newspaper reporting, this misconception was lent credence by the IWW's own colorful rhetoric and avowed revolutionary goals. Only America's forthcoming entry into World War I halted the republication of

• *Deporting IWWs by sea from Marshfield, Oregon.*

Elizabeth Gurley Flynn's well-known pamphlet on sabotage. Four years earlier the major issue leading to Haywood's expulsion from the Socialist Party executive had been his refusal to rule out sabotage and violence as revolutionary options.

Criminal syndicalist laws were sometimes invoked as part of a larger coordinated campaign, but they also operated on a haphazard catch-who-you-can basis. The actual charges were often trivial, the main objective being to get militants out of the workplace and to terrify any workers considering a radical course of action. Keeping Wobblies in local jails on charges that frequently did not hold up in court was almost as disruptive as securing convictions. Wobblies who were convicted usually received sentences that ran into decades, with the actual time served working to between three and five years. When these men and women were finally released or paroled, they returned to a movement in disarray, a period of decline in trade unionism, an IWW spending most of its resources on legal defense.

For employers, a weakened IWW was still a fearsome volcano of possibilities. Just when the IWW seemed totally dormant or at best a harmless rumble, the organization might explode with all its former fury. One such eruption came in the Colorado coalfields in 1927. Partly as a result of agitation concerning the Sacco-Vanzetti case, the IWW was able to lead miners in a strike which simultaneously engaged three major coal areas. The outstanding personality was A.S. Embree, a militant among the Bisbee deportees who had only recently been released from a state prison where he'd been held for criminal syndicalism.

Innovative as ever, the IWW moved singing miners from site to site to bolster picket lines and stage mass rallies. This tactic, called the "car caravan," was later widely used by the United Mine Workers. But the companies responded to this first strike since the Ludlow Massacre of 1913 with new measures of their own, the most spectacular being low-flying airplanes that buzzed outdoor gatherings and picket lines. While the IWW insisted strikers remain non-violent, its opponents recognized no such constraint. On November 21, 1927, the state police machine-gunned a picket line, killing six and wounding twenty-three. In spite of three more killings in 1928, the miners refused to yield. A February settlement granted the only pay hikes for any American coal miners between 1928 and 1930. Since recognition of the IWW as a bargaining unit had never been an issue, the victory had more to do with the courage of individual Wobblies than the viability of their organization.[1]

During the 1930s, the IWW organized hop pickers in the Yakima

Valley of Washington, coal miners in Illinois, construction workers on federal projects such as the Boulder Dam on the Nevada-Arizona border, and industrial home guards in Cleveland, Ohio. But the momentum of the IWW was spent. Whatever small successes it managed were insignificant when compared to the impact of its two major rivals, the Communist Party among would-be revolutionaries and the CIO among industrial trade unionists.

Speculations on various causes for the eclipse of the IWW and on the motivation behind its constant harassment dominate Art Shield's continuing account of his IWW years. His recollections of the Chicago trials and Palmer Raids underscore that one action was aimed at IWW leaders and the other at its actual or potential members. Phil Melman's imprisonment illustrates the arbitrary nature of the enforcement of the criminal syndicalist laws while Art Nurse explains how even the humblest worker became aware of the systematic anti-IWW federal effort. Nicolaas Steelink concludes by offering a vivid contrast of the IWW before and after the suppression by an individual who, following his release from prison, struggled to revive the organization.

Art Shields

I would say that one of the technical factors in the decline of the IWW was that the importance of the migratory worker was greatly lessened with the introduction of various farm machines. Then, when the automobile became common, freight trains were no longer ridden like they once were. That was unfortunate for the IWW, because the Wobblies had learned to control that situation and knew how to organize under those conditions. Technology took that away from them.

Another aspect of the decline was that the IWW had little room for political action after its early years. Bill Haywood used to talk about the two arms of labor: the industrial arm (he'd hold his right arm out) and the political arm (he'd hold out the other). The two go together, he would say. But most of the IWWs did not follow Haywood's thinking on that issue. This became very clear after 1917. Although the IWW welcomed the Russian Revolution at first, as time went on the anarcho-syndicalist element began to criticize and then to attack the Soviet Union. That was destructive. Unity was lost. A lot of people who had been brought to socialist thinking by the IWW left.

One problem that must not be minimized is persecution. At the time the Chicago defendents were sentenced, Ben Fletcher said in a voice that could be heard all over the courtroom that the judge was using bad grammar. Haywood asked what he meant. "His sentences are too long," Fletcher responded. Well, most of those men got sentenced to ten or twenty years and fined from twenty to thirty thousand dollars each. That wasn't very funny. Although the sentences were commuted some years later, they did a lot of damage.

The major charge in the criminal syndicalist laws was that the IWW was violent and destroyed property. While it's true that the Wobblies advocated sabotage, for them that usually meant going slow or prolonging the job. I witnessed that sort of thing in Nome, Alaska, before I went into the army. There was a lot of gold mining around the Bering Sea at that time. The AFL local there had belonged to the old Western Federation of Miners, and the members still had the IWW way of thinking, and some of them

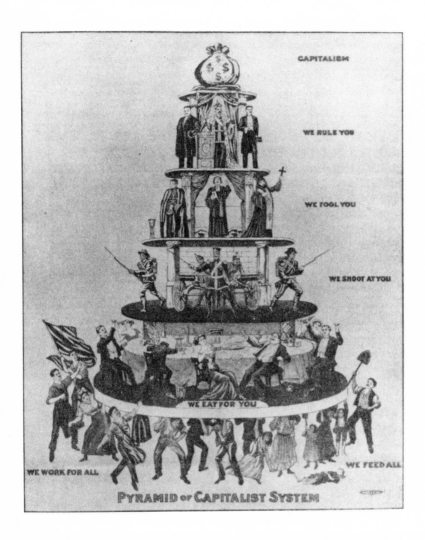

were IWWs on the side. One of those guys was bossing a job to move a mining dredge from one pool in the river to another. This work should not have lasted more than six weeks, but that IWW thinker managed to have it last all winter in order to keep the men employed. That was sabotage as far as the IWW was concerned; but the use of that word didn't do them much good with the general public.

The Palmer Raids were yet another blow to the IWW. These were carried out by J. Edgar Hoover's men, Bureau of Investigation agents. The agency was not then called the Federal Bureau of

Investigation. Senator Welsh, chairman of the Senate Judiciary Committee, estimated that more than ten thousand people were arrested in those raids. These were mainly rank and file workers who would have been prime candidates for membership in radical organizations.

The bosses and government kept after the IWW because it pioneered so many new trails. The IWW was determined to organize the unorganized, whoever they were. In those years before the war, the IWW seemed to be everywhere. The Wobblies definitely had trouble holding workers in their own organizations, but they got the ball rolling for others. Even after it had contracted to a movement of mainly Western workers, it was the one union that took on the copper and construction bosses; and for many years, the IWW remained *the* union of agricultural workers.

Phil Melman

Because of my affiliation with the IWW, I was sent to prison. I was in the Sacramento area at a time when the IWW was organizing. I was in a jungle where the IWWs hung out. Suddenly a bunch of men broke in on us, not police, just business people; but they singled out all of us who had IWW cards and took us to jail. A few months later, we were tried and found guilty of criminal syndicalism. A California law defined criminal syndicalism as any organization that advocated the violent overthrow of the federal or state governments. As long as more than two people were involved, it was a conspiracy. They didn't even attempt to prove we had committed any crimes. They just had a few stool pigeons, men who got paid to testify, to say they belonged to the IWW and did violent sabotage. The question I asked was why we were in jail instead of them. That law was on the books because the farmers demanded it. While I was in San Quentin, a friend of mine went to a meeting in Sacramento where they talked about the criminal syndicalist law. A woman lawyer got up and said that if they didn't retain the law the farmers wouldn't be able to pay the wages being demanded by the agriculture workers and the industry would break down. So it was a question of economics. I was in jail for three years and eleven months.

Art Nurse

My father was a telegraph operator on the Northern Railroad about 30 miles east of Missoula, Montana, where we had a little homestead. I worked around the ranch until I was sixteen and I went to a lumbering camp. That was in 1918 and I joined the IWW right away. We were fighting for the eight-hour day and clean bedding at that time. I didn't much like lumbering and I had itchy feet, so I decided to go to sea. I kept right up until I quit the ships, which was in 1936. Well, I made a couple of trips during the early part of World War II, but I was pretty much finished by 1936.

A problem we always had in organizing was with stool pigeons. I know that in Montana in 1920 in a mining camp, they had a list of every IWW delegate in the whole Northwest pasted on the wall. You could change your name, but the stool pigeons knew who you were. You see, the government had handed over that list to the bosses after they raided our halls. You can figure out that my pride in the government dropped quite a bit when I saw that list. We had never much worried about the government. The IWW had been fighting the bosses, not the government. When the government took sides, you had to think evil of them.

Nicolaas Steelink

I came to the United States because I saw no future in Holland, where I was born. Amsterdam was practically an entire slum, whereas the Hague, where the royalty lived, had palaces. So in 1912, when I was twenty-one years old, I decided to immigrate to America. I was trained as an office worker. I had studied French, English, German, bookkeeping, mathematics and shorthand. I came with the intention to drop all that and become a farmworker and perhaps get my own farm. I landed in Seattle, where I pounded the sidewalks for nine weeks before I got a ten dollar a week job doing clerical work and delivering haberdashery for a department store.

At that time Seattle had many street meetings. There were at least four corners for radicals. Broadway and Eighth was for the socialists and the IWW was at Sixth and Main. Hundreds of people would listen to the soapboxers. The most brilliant speaker I heard was fellow worker Red Doran—William G. Doran. He had everything. If Red Doran had gone to work for the capitalist class, they wouldn't know how much to pay him. Originally, he was a steelworker, one of those guys who makes ingots. He got to be quite an organizer. In 1914, he led a strike in Hollywood against D.W. Griffith, who was making the epic film *Intolerance*. Lots of extras were needed, and the demand was raised for five dollars a day because the work was not steady. Five dollars a day seemed like diamonds then.

The IWW speakers had a poster that showed a pyramid. At the bottom were the workers, by the thousands. Then came the middle class. Then the clergy. Then the military. And on top of that was the emperor or the president. That was a very fine way to propagate the IWW philosophy. We used many tactics. We sang. We had speakers. We put on plays. All of them were connected with the labor movement. The most interesting thing was that when one IWW met another, the greeting was, "Hello, fellow worker." That *fellow worker* was magic. It was used in our meetings: "Fellow worker so-and-so has the floor," and "Fellow worker so-and-so wants to add an amendment to the motion." We were taught to conduct meetings, and everything was recorded and sent to headquarters. A secretary could hold office for a year, but then he had to go back on the job. Of course, some were more efficient than others, and a few, like W.H. Westman, might be Secretary for a lifetime, because they became irreplaceable. But Westman didn't break the rules. He was just re-elected and re-elected. The fundamental thing was that after a year it was time for the secretary to retire. There was quite a fellowship. The most beautiful part was that somebody else called you "fellow worker."

Our attitude toward going to prison was that if they were going to take some, they could take me too. In Sacramento, the charges were so horrible that the defendants refused to take part, refused to have attorneys, refused to testify. They maintained complete silence throughout the trial and were consequently known as the silent defendents. That was during the war. Afterwards they used criminal syndicalist laws against us, which we saw as a rewording of the espionage laws.

As far as the war was concerned, I thought it was futile to come out against it, but I was not going to support it, which is something different. Earlier I'd had a little trouble, because I wouldn't contribute money to someone who came around collecting for a war charity. I thought people were hypocrites. One of the verses of an IWW song summed up my thinking:

Onward, Christian soldiers! Duty's way is plain;
Slay your Christian neighbors, or by them be slain.
Pulpiteers are spouting effervescent swill,
God above is calling you to rob and rape and kill.
All your acts are sanctified by the Lamb on high;
If you love the Holy Ghost, go murder, pray, and die.

In 1919 the Los Angeles branch had at least eight hundred members. We held dances, sent out organizers, and collected money for what we called class war prisoners. We had become very well known in the harvest fields since 1913, when there had been killings during a strike at Marysville and fellow workers had been given life sentences. We had kept up the fight. That fall the local had decided to stage a play and I was to be one of the actors. One night, after my wife had already gone to sleep and I was typing out lines for different roles, there was a knock on the door. When I opened it, I found a man who seemed to be under the influence of liquor. He asked me my name and wanted to know if I belonged to the "Haywood Association." I didn't answer, but he and some others took me out. On the way to jail, they picked up more fellow workers. They seemed to have everyone's address.

We learned later that there were two practicing spies in our local. We also learned that arrests were going on all over the country. These were the Palmer Raids. We were thrown into the drunk tank and it took three days for us to get a hearing. The judge wouldn't let us go on our own recognizance and set the bail at five thousand dollars. Luckily my wife had a socialist lady friend who could put up the money.

Well, in the long run, because of my activities and ideas, I ended up in San Quentin Prison. There was already a number of IWWs there and we met in the yard. I found out I knew very little about the real IWW, even though I had been associated with them for several years. Until I went to prison, I hadn't met the itinerant workers who went from town to town, picking up jobs and living on their own.

After I got out of prison, I was still under surveillance by the government. I viewed myself as a veteran soldier. I thought we would come back and begin to study IWW history and teach the newcomers. I thought that if we had a hundred individuals like myself, we could make an impact. We still had IWW members conducting strikes, but the movement made from 1910 to 1920 had been destroyed. We didn't have enough workers to carry on. When Haywood and the others left the country, they were no longer any good to us. Each time we seemed about to go ahead,

• *IWW headquarters in New York City after raid, November 15, 1919.*

another wave of repression hit us. We just declined. In 1940 I was in Los Angeles and we had eighty members left who came to meetings, but as soon as the war was declared we went down to three. I was lecturing at the time, and I only had the elevator man for an audience. For twenty-two years we couldn't even get into court to determine why we had been put on the subversive list. Truman had done that to us, and it stayed that way through Nixon.

I have remained a very busy man. Hardly half an hour of my time is ever wasted. For everything that I use I try to return something, so it is fifty-fifty. I'm strictly opposed to what we have now. We waste too much time on bookkeeping and on producing and inventing things that are useless and are known to be useless. We cover up the mistakes that are the natural result of the way we do things. I protest all the time—even my wife gets tired of my constant protesting. But I will do that till the day of my death. I never raised my arm against anybody. I never carried a gun. Nor did I ever excuse anyone for carrying a gun. That's not necessary. That doesn't go with me at all. But I criticize everything that I see wrong.

FELLOW WORKERS:

Remember!

WE ARE IN HERE FOR YOU; YOU ARE OUT THERE FOR US

> *For at last we had what it takes*
> *to make songs with.*
> —Kenneth Patchen
> "Joe Hill Listens to
> the Praying"

A BETTER WORLD

The ranks of the IWW were dominated by native-born Americans raised in the traditions of frontier democracy and by immigrants committed to the promises symbolized by the Bill of Rights. These men and women wanted to complete the first American Revolution by extending to all classes the political rights already codified in the Constitution, and they wanted to initiate a second American Revolution which would be dedicated to economic or industrial democracy. This concept of industrial democracy was greatly indebted to the socialist theory that had been developing in Europe for a century. The IWW was especially attracted to ideas prevalent in syndicalism, a socialist trend influenced by anarchist doctrines.

Ben Williams, the first editor of *Solidarity*, had published his translations of French anarcho-syndicalists in the IWW newspaper. Other founders and early leaders of the IWW shared his interest in syndicalist theories, yet even those Wobblies most concerned with the fine points of ideology drew distinctions between the outlook of the IWW and its closest European counterparts.[1] Wobbly opposition to socialism based on state planning or state ownership stemmed less from the fear that a state would abuse such economic power than from the conviction that a socialism directly administered by workers through their unions would be more efficient and democratic. Rather than

• *IWW James P. Thompson at work.*

accepting the anarchists' hostility to any state apparatus, the Wobblies' explanation of the purpose of government was in accord with the sentiments expressed in the American Declaration of Independence. The Wobblies were at home with Henry David Thoreau's belief that the state which governs least governs best, and therefore the state which governed not at all governed best of all. This did not seem much different from Marx's prediction that in time the socialist state would wither away.

In regard to revolutionary tactics and strategies, the IWW insisted that non-democratic means could never produce a democratic society and that a genuine transformation of values could not be entrusted to a small group of highly trained and dedicated individuals. Change must flow from the direct action of millions of workers resolving their needs through democratically operated unions. For the general strike that would end capitalism to be feasible, each industrial union would have to create a constellation of leaders from within its own ranks. Common sense and direct action experience, not abstract ideology or organizational discipline, would distinguish these leaders.

Instead of committing their entire lifetimes to building revolutionary cadres, IWW leaders felt free to take time off to pursue personal goals or simply to allow others experience in leadership positions. Vincent St. John left the IWW to go prospecting, and "Smiling" Joe Ettor went into the wine business. Such drastic shifts generally followed political quarrels; but they could be made in good conscience, because those involved did not believe their active presence would make or break the kind of revolution they envisioned. They also realized that withdrawal from the stress of constant political struggle was a requirement for physical and mental health. In his autobiography, Ralph Chaplin writes of intense periods of political activism alternating with periods devoted to making a living or being with his family. Chaplin notes that when the national IWW leaders were tried in Chicago, it was the first time all of them had ever been together at the same time.

The IWW's vision of a worker-controlled society where civil liberties flourished could not be bound by national frontiers. Unlike the Communist International which insisted on a formal organization of the revolutionary groups active in various countries, the Wobblies believed their view could prevail mainly by the example of their direct actions as reported and explained in reliable publications. The only formal organization outside of the United States undertaken by the IWW was through the Marine Transport Workers Union, which at one time or another had

TENEMOS UN SOLO GRAN ENEMIGO FORMEMOS UNA SOLA GRANDE UNION

UNETE CON NOSOTROS LOS I.W.W.

dozens of locals in foreign ports. The more common connection to the world was through indigenous or national IWW organizations. These came into being in Great Britain (1905), South Africa (1910), Australia (1911), New Zealand (1912), Chile (1919)[2], Mexico (1919)[3], Ecuador (1922), and Canada (1932).[4] Of less direct but immense significance was the impact of IWW deportees and foreigners who associated with the IWW during stays in the United States. One prominent example is James Connolly, who was quite active in the IWW before returning to Ireland where he took part in the Easter Rebellion. Other IWW alumni became major labor leaders in Norway, Spain, Italy, and Great Britain.[5]

The international counterparts most comparable to the movement in the United States were in Australia and Canada. The Australian IWWs were particularly bold in using direct action to oppose World War I. The group also had an adventuristic wing which among other schemes sought to paralyze the capitalist economy by flooding Australia with counterfeit money. In Canada some units were directly affiliated with the American IWW as early as 1906 and others belonged to the One Big Union, an independent Canadian organization whose membership card was interchangeable with that of the IWW. Both groups represented thousands of Canadian workers through the 1930s, but the most dramatic demonstration of American-Canadian solidarity took place in 1912. In response to a strike declared by eight thousand workers on the Canadian Northern, Wobblies on both sides of the border announced a thousand-mile picket line that effectively halted recruitment of strikebreakers as far east as Minneapolis and as far south as San Francisco.

Among the Wobblies anxious to see IWW ideals and IWW history accurately rendered, Tom Scribner and Fred Thompson have been outstanding. Their testimonies can be read as illustrations of how Wobblies who had given much thought to how posterity would view them wanted their beliefs and lives to be judged. Until his death in 1983, Scribner was an activist agitator and something of a counter-culture celebrity in Southern California. His effortless mingling of art and politics and his pervasive sense of humor evoke the buoyant spirit that has always been associated with the IWW. Fred Thompson is the "official" historian of the IWW. He never fails to tell interviewers that when he received approval to do a history in the 1950s, it was "on the understanding that it was not the history of the IWW, but the history of its *first* fifty years."[6]

Tom Scribner

My dad had been in the Knights of Labor, but he didn't like the IWW. He said they were too goddamn radical. Those were the words he used. He said he would never accept the idea that the working class and the employing class had nothing in common. But he knew damn well it was true. In 1912 he took me to a political rally at the Bijou Theater in Duluth, Minnesota. The main speakers were Eugene Victor Debs and Big Bill Haywood. Daniel DeLeon was there, too. It was a campaign to elect Eugene V. Debs president of the United States on the Socialist ticket. My father warned me, "Remember, he's a great speaker, an influential speaker, a good orator, but what he's talking about is just a dream. It can't happen. It'd be a good thing if it could happen, but it can't."
At that time Haywood was still in the Socialist Party and a backer of Debs, whereas most of the Wobblies weren't. The other wing, the anarchists and syndicalists, didn't believe in any kind of political action. They said Debs was just another politician and wouldn't back him. The political wing did, and when the split came, the political wing mainly went into the Communist movement.

I got my first job in vaudeville and my first job in logging in the same year—1914. That was also the year I joined the IWW in the Minnesota woods. Four years before that, when I was just eleven, I saw someone playing a musical saw on a stage in Duluth and I fell in love with the sound and decided I would learn to play it. For two years there I played in vaudeville in the summer and worked in the woods in the winter. Then I left to go to Everett, Washington. All the lumberjacks were going west. They all said the same thing; there's lots of work out west and timber there will last forever. Well, forever is just about over now. Anyways, I just played saw on and off through the years in circus bands, vaudeville bands, dance bands. I worked solo sometimes, but the saw is not really a solo instrument. It's best accompanied by a piano. I also played with guitarists and banjo pickers. The working saw had its origin as a musical instrument about the time of the founding of the republic. It didn't go into decline until around 1921, when the Hawaiian steel guitar came in. I'm still playing it. I'm pretty near eighty years old, so I ain't got a lot of strength left. Mostly I play for labor rallies, picket lines, and protest meetings of one kind or another.

I heard about the Bolshevik Revolution in a logging camp near what is now Valsetz, Oregon. It was 1917. Terrific arguments started every night in the bunkhouse. The chairman of the IWW would get up and open the meeting. He'd bang a work shoe on the table to get attention and say something like, "Gather round here, fellow workers. We've got a goddamn revolution to talk about." That chairman happened to be one of the pro-political faction, so he'd say, "The Russkies beat us to it and we've got to re-examine what we're doing and see where we're short. The fact is that they've done the trick and we're still talking." Then someone from the opposite side would grab him by the shirt and say, "Sit down, you Big Hoosier, you don't know what you're talking about." It was fast and furious. Generally, it'd break up with fist fights. I was only eighteen then and I'll tell you I was shy of those slab-sided lumberjacks.

In those days I believed in the Debs dream, a socialist world without war or police. I still think it's going to take several generations to breed greed out of people. The only way that can be done is by changing the methods of production. The methods of production determine human nature in any country. You have a capitalist method in this country, and there's more at stake here than anywhere else. As a result you have the most savage ruling class in the world.

That savagery was obvious in the lumber camps. There were lots of accidents. I had seven major accidents which sent me to the hospital with broken arms, legs, and ribs. One time a log rolled up my chest. It broke four bones and I could feel it squeezing my insides loose. My insides fell out of my tail end and hung way down to the tops of my cork shoes. Twenty years later I saw the nurse who took care of me. She was surprised to see me still alive and still working in a saw mill. She said the doctor had to stuff my intestines back in like they were rope, curling them and shoving them back up inside of me. I also had a finger cut off in a rig. I fell headfirst toward the saw and had the choice to take it on the head or throw up a hand. Well, the Wobblies were concerned with safety issues. They led the fight against the brake block, which was particularly dangerous. It was outlawed.

There was a group in the IWW that we called the sabcats and the blackcats and names like that. They believed in wrecking machinery. We used to argue with them saying, "You guys are crazy. You're blowing up and destroying equipment we'll have to rebuild when we take over. We want to organize these workers and take over the means of production, not destroy them."

Your people of today think corruption is a new phenomenon in unions, but the leaders of labor have always served as lieutenants of the capitalist class within the ranks of the workers. You pay a union officer seventy-five thousand or more a year, and he's going to look after his own best interests and those of the stockholders of the companies he's involved with. As far as the AF of L goes, in the old days, they told us: a fair day's wage for a fair day's work. The IWW countered: organize the working class to take over the means of production and create a new society in the shell of the old. The AF of L wanted no part of that proposition, I can tell you. We used to call Gompers, "old Sell'em Out Sam."

In my estimation, the best tactic that came out of the IWW was slowing production. That brought bosses to their knees quicker than anything else. General strikes were effective, too. We had

• *Agricultural workers band, Midwest.*

an important one in 1917 that spread up and down the Pacific Coast. I was in Seattle then and we would get calls for help. Twenty-five of us would load into cars and go strengthen a picket line in some other town. We were roving pickets. In that area, it was more or less a movement of single men. The big demand we won was the eight-hour day. The Knights of Labor had failed to get it and so had the AF of L. Oh, the owners tried to stop us anyway they could. They created a spruce division in the army. They'd draft a logger, maybe he was a bucker or a faller, and they'd put him in the woods to work alongside a man who was getting civilian pay. The civilian was drawing ten to fifteen dollars a day, and the poor devil from the army was getting thirty dollars a month.

I continued in logging until 1967; that's about fifty-three years total. I was blacklisted in 1916 and that held until 1935, when the Wagner Act illegalized blacklists. At least it was supposed to. They still used them, but it had to be underground after that. If I worked in camps before that time, I'd be John Steele or John Bloke or whatever; any name would do. After the IWW I joined the American Communist Party. I stayed until the middle 1940s. I would say that pursuing the IWW line now would be an exercise in futility, because half of the battle is won: the building of industrial unions. Now that we have them, let's repair them. But in the old days the IWW was the most relevant union, the most militant. We got results. And we had fun. We had little two-by-four-inch stickers gummed on the back that you wet and put up. One read, "Trust in the Lord and sleep in the street." Another was, "Jesus saves the willing slaves." People were afraid of us, because they figured we were a bunch of roughnecks, "I Won't Works," "I Want Whisky," and all that. One thing was true: we wouldn't work unless we got decent treatment.

Here in Santa Cruz, some people are erecting a statue of me playing the musical saw. There's been quite a hassle about it in the city council and in the papers, but they finally got permission to put it up in the mall opposite the town clock. Ordinarily, a statue would show a man on a horse with a sword drawn ready to kill some s.o.b. Mine shows a man playing a musical saw. That bronze is supposed to last five thousand years. I can just visualize someone in the future asking, "What is that man doing?" Well, he's playing a musical saw." "What's a saw?" "That's something you cut wood with." "What's wood?"

Another unusual thing is that everyone knows that I'm an avowed communist, and those who are avowed are the worst kind. Of course, the winds of political change could blow and that statue could go to the city dump. I can't worry about that. I'm still playing the old songs and campaigning to make the musical saw popular again. I don't know how far I'm going to get, but I'll play for as long as my health and time permit. I'm going to cut a record in Hollywood and make a movie in Santa Monica. After that I can get back to the job of overthrowing the government. I'll keep reminding people that Thomas Jefferson said we should have a revolution every twenty years or so and that Henry Wallace said this is the century of the common man. So perchance if you are around Santa Cruz you will see a statue of a man wearing a derby hat and playing the musical saw in one hand and holding the *Communist Manifesto* in the other. That will be me—Tom Scribner.

Fred Thompson

My life has been shaped by the fact that in my childhood I suffered from bronchitis and had to spend a large part of the year indoors. I became an avid reader. You might even say I'm sort of a bookworm radical. I was born in Canada, in St. John, New Brunswick, in 1900, and I would say my radicalism was tripped off by something I read in the fall of 1913. A headline in the local newspaper announced an abundant harvest. I was very happy, for my family had known quite a bit of poverty and I knew many people who I thought would now be better off. I discussed this with my family and found things were not so simple. A brother of mine who was studying for the ministry knew a bit of economics and explained to me how the system worked. That made me look up "economics" in the encyclopedia we had. The article talked about what Adam Smith had written in *The Wealth of Nations*. I got a copy of the book and read it. I found out about Malthus, and then I came across a reference to socialist criticism of Smith and Malthus. I ran into a book by John Stuart Mill and found out about utopian socialists. I got ideas from Saint-Simon and Fourier. I did this reading over the course of a year.

In 1914 Canada became involved in the First World War. Big recruiting posters stated that king and country needed young men. Then I heard that a socialist had been arrested for saying the king was a parasite and that the king and the country were bleeding us. I had felt pretty much the same thing, so when the socialist came to trial, I went to the courthouse. I discovered there was a real live Socialist Party that had meetings every Sunday at the Labor Temple. Previously, I had thought of Socialists as belonging to the 1840s. I started to attend their affairs and wanted to join, but I had to wait until I was sixteen before I could become a member. I soon became secretary and handled mail from various left-wing organizations. The trials of the IWW were written about in many publications, but the first piece of IWW literature I ever read was *With Drops of Blood*, a pamphlet written by Bill Haywood. It gave an account of how the IWWs had been mistreated, jailed and killed.

The Lid Can't Last Much Longer

In 1920 I left St. John to work in western Canada, where I joined the One Big Union. The nucleus of this effort was a group of AF of L unions in Winnipeg. They wanted to drop their craft structure and organize industrially, but their overall perspective was more like the British labor movement than the IWW. What I heard about the IWW was allegations that they were a bunch of nuts who went around burning down wheatfields and haystacks. When I came into the United States in 1922, I just worked around on different jobs up and down the Pacific Coast. I traveled by freight trains, slept in jungles, and mixed here and there with Wobblies. I soon concluded that they were really a bunch of common sense working stiffs. While I was working in the building trades in San Francisco, I joined.

I became involved with various activities, and it happened that I stopped off in Marysville, California, to pass out some newspapers. I didn't plan on getting arrested, but I had hardly given any papers out before the police grabbed me and charged me with a felony. You see, in 1913 that town had a strike by 2,800 hop pickers. The father of the then-current district attorney had been slain and Wobblies were blamed for the killing. The original charge they put on me was changed to criminal syndicalism when they found a job delegate's rigging in my hip pocket. All that amounted to was credentials for collecting dues and issuing membership cards. Well, I was tried for criminal syndicalism, but the jury could not come to an unanimous verdict. They tried me again in the fall, with two other Wobblies they had picked up. We were all found guilty. I went to San Quentin Prison on November 7, 1923, the anniversary of the Bolshevik Revolution. I did not get out until March 7, 1927.

When I got to San Quentin, there were already about one hundred other IWWs in there. We set to work to improve the job. The porridge had maggots in it and we had to eat beans every day. We did some agitation and held strikes. The authorities locked us up, put us in the hole, and gave us a diet of bread; but eventually we won improvements in food, recreation, and health services.

The IWW always used humor in its activities, and San Quentin was no exception. There was a guy there called Baldy Stewart who had three hairs on the top of his head. One of the most miserable aspects of being in there was that we had to line up for everything: to eat, to work, to go to the library, whatever. We were always in line and it got really bad in rainy weather. Old Baldy used to take the edge off by pulling out a little pocket mirror and comb. He'd fuss over how to part those three hairs. Should he put two on one side and one on the other? No, maybe he should just comb them all back. He could fiddle around with those three hairs for the longest time. It wasn't just to amuse himself; it made things easier for all of us. A good part of our humor was of that nature: to make you laugh that you may not weep.

Our humor was usually aimed at some absurdity in the system or at delusions a working stiff might have. We'd say some working stiffs were capitalists from ears up, workers from the ears down. We'd call a guy like that a "Scissorbill" or, if he was really dumb, "Mr. Block."

Soapboxers used humor to develop complex ideas for their audiences. Parables and fables were always well-received. One of the most effective was about the cormorant, a bird with a rather large bill for catching fish. IWW speakers told how the Japanese fisherman would tie a cord around its neck so the cormorant could not swallow. As soon as the bird caught a fish, the fisherman would use the cord to pull the bird back to where they were waiting. All the bird got was a few less savory pieces, like the guts, head, and tail. The cormorant would still be hungry so it would go out fishing again, and the whole process would be repeated.

The story goes that the cormorants learned to speak Japanese. They got indignant about the tiny share they were getting and organized the Protective Association of Cormorants. The Japanese Fisherman's Association balked at the idea of higher wages, but finally agreed to give them little pieces of paper that could be put under a rock until the end of a day. Then the cormorant could buy as much fish as they had paper for. Guts cost so many pieces, tails so much, and so on. The cormorants found things had not really changed, so they decided they had to go on strike, even at the risk of dying from hunger. Their demand was for a ten percent increase in paper. By the time the strike was settled, the cormorants found that on account of the fish shortages, prices had gone up. The fisherman also explained to them that the cost of cords and neck rings had risen. A Wobbly cormorant stood up and said that the cord and ring system should be abolished and that cormorants didn't have to deal with the fishermen at all. But the union leaders said we must not attack the basic social system in which we all live. They settled for another round of increases in the slips of paper.

That parable was told and retold. Soapboxers would also recite poems. One I heard a lot was "To Labor," by Charlotte Perkins Gilman, who was renown for her work in the woman's suffrage movement and was a socialist. The Wobbly papers often had four-line poems that rhymed. What we used most of all was song. If you will analyze the words of "Solidarity Forever," you will see it is practically a restatement of the IWW preamble. A good many of our songs were humorous and gained circulation far beyond our ranks. We belonged to a tradition of singing that is rooted in a time prior to mass media, to when music was disseminated very largely by guys who played in taverns, or saloons, as they were called. Almost every town had a few major saloons that working stiffs frequented and where the piano player introduced the latest songs. A tune could get around the country almost as rapidly as it can today. Joe Hill's song about Casey Jones was very popular and got heard in vaudeville and saloons as well as at labor events.

Most people understand that the basic difference between the IWW and the AF of L was that of industrial versus craft unionism. What they do not understand is how that difference used to work out. The development of a national labor movement was more or less by happenstance and resulted in a federation of craft unions, each guarding its own jurisdiction. Demography played a big role with the result that a national or local union might be of only one religion, political view or nationality. There might be a Swedish carpenters local in the same place as a German carpenters local. Even though they made speeches in favor of brotherly love, only the right nationality could work in that particular local. I recall in my early days working in the building trades in San Francisco that I only could work on the Masonic Temple because they thought I was a Protestant. Later on, I worked on the Cathedral of St. Peter and St. Paul because they thought I was a Catholic. That kind of thing was fairly common in those days.

The whole reason for the IWW coming into existence was the evolution of modern industry had made the craft system obsolete. Workers had to organize on the same basis that they were hired on. Workers had to be free from discrimination because of the polyglot nature of the labor force. Structure has a lot to do with how a worker perceives the world. What does we mean when one speaks of a union? The AF of L pattern was to think of we as metal polishers. Later, many of the CIO unions that filed as industrial unions actually included people working in one plant who happened to practice unionism together. For them, we meant the workers in this one place. A union has to be on guard against plant consciousness and craft consciousness, as opposed to class consciousness. Sometimes they even include management in the we referring to a plant or industry. The IWW was very clear in stating we meant everyone that worked.

The IWW soapboxers would emphasize that a capitalist would never come to scab. The scab was always another worker. Thus, there was no reason to be afraid of a capitalist or a politician or anyone like that. The only person to fear is the fellow worker who might take the job when you were on strike. At first, carpenters only needed to fear those other carpenters who lived nearby. As transportation became more evolved, there had to be an alliance with carpenters in all the towns in the region. If the work was something that could be moved around, all who did such work had to be organized. The answer to this problem was solidarity. Terence Powderly, head of the old Knights of Labor, used the slogan, "An injury to one is a concern of all." He said he found that phrase in a letter an unknown person had sent to a labor paper. The IWW took over the idea and changed it to: "An injury to one is an injury to all."

Generally, the IWW is considered to have been a Western or Northwestern union. If you look at the records, where the dues came from and where the strikes were, in the years up to World War I there was more action east of the Mississippi than west.

We had our first successful textile workers strike in Skowhegan, Maine, in 1907. The major organizer of the textile union was James P. Thompson. I'm often asked if he was a relative. He wasn't. Thompson was from the old school of the nineteenth century. He could talk to people who didn't speak English by using body language, expressions, and acting. One routine he used was to compare each local to a joint in the finger, and each national union to a whole finger, and one big union to be the clenched fist. Another thing he would do was to show how the fingers might be used together to pick things up as well as to make a fighting fist. He had a skit where instead of people going to the boss to ask about wages and conditions, the boss had to call in a union secretary. He had quite a monologue worked out regarding that conversation between the boss and the union secretary. Thompson liked to give these talks at noon, during a break for lunch, and he was very effective.

In evaluating what happened in the East and the West, we can

• *IWW rally in Sidney, Australia.*

see that sometimes our rhetoric was not discrete. Sometimes we engaged in strikes or activities that tended to weaken us rather than build us up. There were instances where we could have built up the treasury and increased membership in the way traditional unions did, but when people called for help, we usually responded. It's also easy to forget the victories we won. After Lawrence, wages and conditions improved all over New England. Friends of mine who work on the ore boats in Lake Superior tell me that the safety equipment now used is virtually the same we struck for and won in 1913. In hard rock mining the addition of wet drills and the two-man safety rule was due to the IWW. We could go industry by industry to show similar gains.

Many tactics we pioneered became part of the arsenal of the labor movement. We expanded the idea of what a picket line could be and staged sit-down strikes. The shop steward system seen in many industries is the outgrowth of the job delegate system developed by our agricultural workers. The emphasis now heard about improving conditions as well as raising wages is a development of what the IWW has been saying all along. We were not the only ones with ideas like these, or even the originators of them all; but we usually expressed and fought for the most advanced thoughts of our fellow workers.

When considering the history of the IWW, I think it is important to understand that we set out to do something that is much more difficult than anything ever done by anybody anywhere. That we haven't yet succeeded in abolishing the capitalist system should not be a surprise. We didn't invent the idea that the workers of the world have to stick together, but we have been its champions to a much greater degree than other unions. We believe that the realities of production force us to a global view. Otherwise unemployment will just be transferred from country to country.

Unions have retained the focus of being the collective peddlers of labor power, arrangers of wages and conditions. The IWW always understood that this means that beneath every transaction is the fact that one class is telling the other class what to do. The path we are going on now—the "fast buck road" is what the preachers call it—is the road to destruction. I do not speak of the future of the unions, but of the human race. We produce things to kill each other rather than to help each other. The IWW believes that labor should put out its own plan about what to do with the world. We would transfer the available resources into what will satisfy human needs. We don't need to produce things people don't want and then try to convince them through Madison Avenue advertising that they do want them. We don't need to continue to support a culture which makes combustion engines that deplete resources faster than necessary. We don't need to cut down trees to make newspaper pages to tell people to shop at this store instead of that one. We don't need to build skyscrapers that shut off the breezes on Lake Michigan when we could be building houses that people need. The greater part of the work which we do need not be done at all.

Solidarity Forever

by Ralph Chaplin

(Sung to the tune of *John Brown's Body*)

When the Union's inspiration through the workers blood shall
    run,
There can be no power greater anywhere beneath the sun.
Yet what force on earth is weaker than the feeble strength of
    one?
But the Union makes us strong.

> *Solidarity forever!*
> *Solidarity forever!*
> *Solidarity forever!*
> *For the Union makes us strong.*

Is there aught we hold in common with the greedy parasite
Who would lash us into serfdom and would crush us with his
    might?
Is there anything left to us but to organize and fight?
For the Union makes us strong.   *[chorus]*

It is we who plowed the prairies; built the cities where they
    trade;
Dug the mines and built the workshops; endless miles of
    railroad laid.
Now we stand outcast and starving, 'midst the wonders we
    have made;
But the Union makes us strong.   *[chorus]*

All the world that's owned by idle drones is ours and ours
    alone.
We have laid the wide foundations; built it skyward stone by
    stone.
It is ours, not to slave in, but to master and to own,
While the Union makes us strong.   *[chorus]*

They have taken untold millions that they never toiled to
    earn,
But without our brain and muscle not a single wheel can
    turn.
We can break their haughty power; gain our freedom when
    we learn
That the Union makes us strong.   *[chorus]*

In our hands is placed a power greater than their hoarded
    gold;
Greater than the might of armies, magnified a thousand-fold.
We can bring to birth a new world from the ashes of the old.
For the Union makes us strong.   *[chorus]*

THE HARVEST DRIVE IS ON AGAIN!

The Industrial Pioneer

An Illustrated Labor Magazine
July, 1925   Price 20 cents

BIBLIOGRAPHY

The most comprehensive bibliographic guide to the IWW is to be found in Joseph Conlin, ed., *At the Point of Production—The Local History of the IWW* (Westport, CT: Greenwood Press, 1982), pp. 238-318. The bibliography was compiled by Dione Miles, archivist at the Walter P. Reuther Library, Wayne State University, Detroit, Michigan. The bibliography is divided into categories of Research Archives, Federal and State Documents, IWW Publications, IWW Pamphlets, Related Non-IWW Pamphlets, Doctoral Dissertations, Master's Essays and Theses, Articles and Books. An item not included in this bibliography is a microfilm source on repression of the IWW, *U.S. Military Intelligence Reports: Surveillance of Radicals in the United States, 1917-1941* (Frederick, Maryland: University Publications of America, 1984). Fully a third of the 34 reels focus directly on the IWW while other reels are also related.

General readers will find the following three histories of interest. Joyce L. Kornbluh, *Rebel Voices—An IWW Anthology* (Ann Arbor, MI: University of Michigan Press, 1972) provides informative lead essays to a rich collection of IWW writing and graphics. Philip S. Foner, *The Industrial Workers of the World—1905-1917* (New York: International Publishers, 1965) offers a detailed account of the period with a decided sympathy for the IWW's revolutionary aims. This is the fourth volume of Foner's *History of the Labor Movement in the United States*. Other volumes in the series also contain references to the IWW. Melvyn Dubofsky, *We Shall Be All* (New York: Quadrangle, 1969) is exceptionally strong in providing background to the formation of the IWW but is thin on post-1917 events.

Among IWW autobiographical works, two give a vivid sense of the times and organization. They are Elizabeth Gurley Flynn, *The Rebel Girl* (New York: International Publishers, 1955) and Ralph

Chaplin, *Wobbly: The Rough and Tumble Story of a Radical* (Chicago: University of Chicago press, 1949). William D. Haywood, *The Autobiography of Big Bill Haywood* (New York: International Publishers, 1929) concentrates on his career in the Western Federation of Miners. There is some question whether the book, written by an ailing Haywood in Moscow, is entirely his own work, but this is most definitely not his finest writing.

The endnotes which follow sometimes contain annotated bibliographic entries for additional reading on the specific topic. The citation form followed is to give complete bibliographic entries for books the first time listed and provide only author's last name and the title thereafter. Songs quote in the text have been taken from various edition of *The Little Red Song Book*. Also useful was Kornbluh, *Rebel Voices*. Readers should be aware that some songs have variations in what has been a continuing oral tradition. The exact selection of songs in any given edition of *The Little Red Song Book* gives a sense of what the organization was most concerned with at the time. Thus, the 1918 edition, issued at the time of America's entry into World War I, deleted eighteen songs about sabotage and revolution. In the edition which was issued in 1984, considerable space is given to songs printed for the first time in order to emphasize what the organization considers the living presence of the IWW.

The interviews in this book (with the exception of the one with George Hodin) were done by Stewart Bird and Deborah Shaffer for *The Wobblies*. They made transcripts of these interviews which were then edited by Dan Georgakas. The edited versions were reviewed by Bird and Shaffer and when possible by those who had been interviewed. The George Hodin interview was done by Dan Georgakas expressly for this book and was reviewed by Hodin. The raw transcripts from which the oral histories were shaped have been donated to the Oral History of the American Left Project of the Tamiment Library, New York University, New York City. These transcripts contain considerable material that was not used in this book or in *The Wobblies*. The introductions to each section were written by Georgakas with assistance from Bird and Shaffer.

The sources for the graphics and photographs used in this book include the Industrial Workers of the World, the Seattle Historical Society, the Everett Public Library, the State Historical Society of Wisconsin, the Colorado Historical Society, the Minnesota Historical Society, the University of Nevada Library (Special Collections), Wayne State University (Archives of Labor), the Arizona Historical Society, the University of Washington Library, the International Museum of Photography (George Eastman House), the Chicago Historical Society, and the Paterson Library.

NOTES

THE IWW RECONSIDERED

[1] See Joe Murphy's discussion of the most commonly cited explanations for the origin of the nickname "Wobbly," p.50.

[2] See bibliographic notes preceding these endnotes. Some readers may also be interested in the dispute about the importance of Joe Hill and his possible guilt in the murder for which he was executed. Wallace Stegner and Vernon H. Jensen have expressed the view that Hill may have been a murderer and a thug unworthy of his legend. Their argument has been assailed by the IWW, Philip S. Foner, and Barrie Stavis among others. Relevant readings follow. Critical of Joe Hill: Wallace Stegner, "I Dreamed I Saw Joe Hill Last Night," *Pacific Spectator*, January 1947; Stegner, "Joe Hill: The Wobblies' Troubadour," *The New Republic*, January 5, 1948; Stegner, *The Preacher and the Slave* (New York: Doubleday & Co., 1950), a novel; and Vernon H. Jensen, "The Legend of Joe Hill," *Industrial and Labor Relations Review* 5.4 (April, 1951), pp. 356-366. Supportive of Hill's innocence and importance: IWW edited response in *The New Republic*, November 15, 1948, and in complete form in *Industrial Worker*, November 13, 1948; Philip S. Foner, *The Case of Joe Hill* (New York: International publishers, 1965); and Barrie Stavis, *The Man Who Never Died* (South Brunswick, NJ: A.S. Barnes & Co., 1972), a play containing an introduction relevant to this issue. Since publishing that edition, Stavis has collected considerable additional material establishing Hill's significance as an organizer and further shredding the flimsy murder charge. The playwright was kind enough to let Dan Georgakas examine some of this material, which will eventually be published in what should be the definitive word on this subject.

[3] *The Wobblies*, 89 minutes, color. Directed by Stewart Bird and Deborah Shaffer. Researchers: Pierce Rafferty, Erika Gottfried, and Peter Smallman. Premiered at the New York Film Festival, 1979. Distributed by First Run Features of New York City.

[4] Facsimile edition of *Proceedings: The Founding Convention of the IWW* (New York: Merit Publishers, 1969).

[5] The Socialist Party, an outgrowth of organizations and trends originating in the nineteenth century, was founded in 1905 and reached an electoral high point in 1912 when its presidential candidate, Eugene V. Debs, polled over 900,000 votes, or six percent of total ballots cast. In that year, the Party had 118,000 dues-paying members and 1,200 of those members held some public office. Socialist electoral totals and totals for other radical parties can be traced in *Presidential Elections Since 1789* (Washington, DC: Congressional Quarterly, 1983).

[6] American novelists, playwrights, and poets have frequently included loving portraits of the IWW in their work. One of the first to do so was Upton Sinclair in his play *Singing Jailbirds*, which was staged in Greenwich Village with the assistance of John Dos Passos and Eugene O'Neill, soon to record their own appreciations of the IWW. Just a few of the authors who have written about the IWW and are not cited elsewhere in this book are E.L. Doctorow, Theodore Dreiser, Meridel Le Sueur, Clancy Sigal, Kenneth Rexroth, William Carlos Williams, and Harry Mark Petrakis. Two docu-novels of historical accuracy are: Robert Houston, *Bisbee '17* (New York: Pantheon, 1979) and Thomas Churchill, *Centralia Dead March* (Willimantic, CT: Curbstone Press, 1980). A docu-drama featuring IWW legal cases was written by Stewart Bird and Peter Robilotta, *The Wobblies—The U.S. versus W.D. Haywood et. al.*, (New York: Smyrna Press, 1980). Barrie Stavis' *The Man Who Never Died* has been translated into a dozen languages and was adapted as an opera with music by Alan Bush and libretto by Stavis.

[7] Len De Caux, *The Living Spirit of the Wobblies* (New York: International Publishers, 1978), p. 138.

[8] Kornbluh, *Rebel Voices*, contains several IWW songs specifically advocating violence: "When the Leaves Come out," by Ralph Chaplin, p. 299, and "Ta-Ra-Ra-Boom De-Ay" by Joe Hill, p. 143, are two examples. Direct references to use of the *sabot*

are found in "Saw Mill 'Accidents,' " by Wooden Shoe Kid, p. 56, and "The Rebel's Toast," by Joe Hill, p. 57.

[9] Louis Adamic, *Dynamite—The Story of Class Violence in America*, rev. ed. (Gloucester, MA: Peter Smith, 1963) provides considerable material on this subject. Also see pertinent sections in Dubofsky, *We Shall Be All*.

[10] Documents from and commentary on nine free speech battles are collected in Philip S. Foner, *Fellow Workers and Friends— The IWW Free-Speech Fights as Told By Participants* (Westport, CT: Greenwood Press, 1981). His *Industrial Workers of the World* also contains extensive coverage of various free speech fights.

[11] The Second Socialist International, a loose confederation of autonomous political parties of many nations, was established in 1889 and considered itself the direct heir of the International Workingman's Association founded in 1869 by Karl Marx and associates.

[12] Dubofsky, *We Shall Be All*, pp. 398-444 and related endnotes, provides devastating documentation of the federal conspiracy against the IWW.

[13] H.C. Peterson and Gilbert C. Fite, *Opponents of War—1917-1918* (Madison, WI: University of Wisconsin Press, 1967), p. 19. This work is an excellent source of information on the wider effort against radicals during the time period indicated.

[14] Norman A. Graebner, Gilbert C. Fite, and Philip L. White, *A History of the American People*, volume 2 (New York: McGraw-Hill Book Co. 1971), p. 958.

[15] Some three thousand deportation warrants were served in thirty-three states and at least five hundred actual deportations took place. A sense of the brutality of the raids can be obtained by reviewing events in Detroit where twenty-eight halls and meeting places were struck and eight hundred persons held. For nearly a week the prisoners had no bedding, no legal representations, and only one drinking fountain and one bathroom. Family members were beaten within sight of the prisoners and on one occasion police fired shots that wounded one of the detained. Mayor James Couzens was moved to condemn the situation as "intolerable in a civilized city." Even more

significant than the immediate physical intimidation of those actually detained was the chilling effect on the political rights of the foreign born. Theodore Draper, *The Roots of American Communism* (New York: Viking Press, 1957), p. 207, notes that the organizations composing the nascent Communist movement fell from a collective membership of sixty thousand before the raids to ten thousand afterwards.

16 De Caux, *The Living Spirit*, p. 138.

17 At the time the IWW came into existence, many Americans used *anarchism* and *socialism* as nearly interchangeable terms. Even those more sensitive to the specific anarchist tradition often blurred significant differences between competing schools of anarchism. Wobblies were attracted to those anarchist currents that stressed non-authoritarian structures such as cooperatives, collectives, federations, innovative schools, and decentralized industrial unions. They were hostile to more individualistic anarchists with whom they often had bitter disputes. They also came to a total rejection of Marxism-Leninism, which they identified as the practices visible in the Soviet Union and its ideological supporters. A fascinating account of Wobbly volunteer workers who found it impossible to adjust to the political and economic system taking shape early in the history of the USSR can be found in J.P. Morray, *Project Kuzbas* (New York: International Publishers, 1983). The project involved an experiment to develop the coal, chemical industries and agriculture of the Kuznetsk Basin (Kuzbas) of Siberia from 1921 to 1926.

18 See *Business Week*, January 6, 1945, pp. 96-98, for a sense of the alarm the IWW could still cause at such a late date in its history. *Time*, April 1, 1946, p. 25, was more scoffing while Dan Wakefield, "The Haunted Hall: The IWW at Fifty," *Dissent* 5.5 (Fall, 1956), p. 414, was sympathetic. *The Wall Street Journal* of August 17, 1983, considered the IWW worthy of a front page story under the headline: "For the 'Wobblies,' A Shaky Economy Aids in 'Comeback.' "

19 Daniel Guérin, *One Hundred Years of Labor in the USA* (London: Links, 1979). See especially his discussion of the Taft-Hartley Law, p. 161, and the Landrum-Griffin Act, p. 195.

FANNING THE FLAMES

[1] This observation by muckraker Ray Stannard Baker, "The Revolutionary Strike," *The American Magazine* 54.1 (May 1912), p. 24, irrevocably established this distinctive feature of the IWW in the public mind. Nearly all historians of the IWW have drawn upon his coverage of the strike.

[2] Chaplin, *Wobbly*, p. 207.

[3] Quoted by Kornbluh, *Rebel Voices*, p. 71.

[4] Covington Hall, "In Defense of Dreaming," reprinted in *Free Spirits: Annals of the Insurgent Imagination*, volume 1 (San Francisco: City Lights Books, 1982), edited by Paul Buhle, Jayne Cortez, Philip Lamantia, et. al. Also informative is the accompanying biography of Hall by David Roediger, pp. 178-181.

[5] Program notes provided by Bruce Phillips, 1983.

BINDLESTIFFS

[1] One need go no farther than John Steinbeck's *Grapes of Wrath*, dealing with agricultural workers of the 1930s, or Edward R. Murrow's television exposé *Harvest of Shame*, dealing with agricultural workers of the 1950s, to see that agricultural unions were still desperately needed many years after the "mechanization" of harvesting. Not until the 1960s was the United Farm Workers Union able to gain recognition in some areas. Even then, despite massive support by the AFL-CIO and the Roman Catholic Church, the successes were modest.

[2] Foner, *The Industrial Workers of the World*, p. 478.

WOMEN IN TEXTILES

[1] On May 4, 1886, in Chicago's Haymarket Square, a bomb exploded as police began to disperse a political rally. Fifty-six persons were wounded and seven left dead. Eight anarchists were charged as being responsible for the bomb and subsequently convicted. Four were executed, one allegedly committed suicide

in his cell, and three were imprisoned until an 1893 parole. Few historians now doubt the innocence of these men. The Haymarket incident led to the establishment of May 1 as a day to demonstrate labor's strength.

[2] Meredith Tax, *The Rising of the Women* (New York: Monthly Review Press, 1980), pp. 134-138, deals with the efforts of IWW Jane Street to organize housemaids.

[3] Steven Golin, "The Paterson Pageant: Success or Failure?" *Socialist Review* (May/June 1983), pp. 45-78, offers an upbeat interpretation of the event emphasizing the interaction of artist-intellectuals and workers.

THE HOME GUARD

[1] Fred W. Thompson and Patrick Murfin, *The IWW—Its First Seventy Years, 1905-1975* (Chicago: IWW, 1976), pp. 166-69, deals with the last major IWW effort in auto during the early 1930s. This drive featured the sitdown strike, a tactic used to greater effect by the CIO a few years later. The IWW failure in auto caused many long-time Detroit members to leave the organization for more conventional unions. Most prominent of these was John Pancner, who had been one of the Chicago defendants. A study of ten IWWs who substantially influenced the early United Auto Workers appeared in the Spring 1982 issue of *Detroit in Perspective: The Journal of the Detroit Historical Society*, and was commented upon by Fred Thompson in *Industrial Worker* (October 1982), p. 6.

[2] De Caux, *The Living Spirit*, p. 143.

[3] James P. Cannon, *The First Ten Years of American Communism* (New York: Pathfinder Press, 1962) contains two relevant essays. The most important is "The IWW—The Great Anticipation," pp. 277-310. Also interesting is "Eugene V. Debs and the Socialist Movement of His Time," pp. 245-76. Cannon left the IWW to become a leading figure in the early Communist Party of America. He was a founder of the Socialist Workers Party and national chairman emeritus until his death in 1974. Arne Swabeck was another individual who moved from the IWW to the CPUSA to the Trotskyist movement. A short biography of him by Mark Lause with his reflections on the Seattle general strike is found in *Free Spirits*, pp. 182-186.

TIMBERBEASTS

[1] During the time he was most active in the IWW, John Miller was usually known as Jack Leonard, a combination of an alternative first name and his middle name. His "Jails Didn't Make Them Weaken" first printed in *Industrial Worker*, October 30, 1946, has been republished often and bears the name Jack Leonard.

HARD ROCK MINING

[1] A yellow dog contract requires an employee to resign from or refrain from joining a union. Yellow dog contracts were made illegal by the Norris-LaGuardia Act of 1932.

[2] No other major American novelist has written so often about the IWW as Dos Passos. His *USA* trilogy amounts to an IWW eulogy developed through fictional characters and poetic biographies of Bill Haywood, Joe Hill, Wesley Everest, Eugene Debs, and John Reed. Other Dos Passos novels treat the IWW favorably as do his autobiographical writings and articles about specific political causes, such as the effort to aid the Harlan County miners in the 1930s. Although Dos Passos did not think the IWW approach could prevail, he always lauded its moral vision. Even after a political turn to the right marked by a fierce denunciation of the Communist Party, Dos Passos stood by his original evaluation of the Wobblies.

CIVIL LIBERTIES FOR ALL

[1] Quoted in an extensive discussion of the IWW position on racism by Foner, *The Industrial Workers of the World*, p. 125.

[2] Tax, *The Rising of the Women*, pp. 125-63, is devoted in large part to the sexual rights issue and the IWW. Among IWW leaders, Bill Haywood and Ben Williams tended to be the most supportive of feminist concerns. For fascinating comments on how the IWW interacted with women interested in reproductive rights, Margaret Sanger, *An Autobiography* (New York: Dover Publications, 1971), is essential.

[3] Nancy Krieger, "Queen of the Bolsheviks: The Hidden History of Dr. Marie Equi," *Radical America* 17.5 (September/October, 1983), pp. 55-73, provides considerable material on Equi's IWW involvement.

[4] Joe Hill had asked that his body be reduced to ashes and thrown to the breezes to help flowers grow. He further requested that no part of his body should remain in Utah. On November 19, 1916, the first anniversary of his execution, Bill Haywood presented envelopes with Hill's ashes to IWW delegates and fraternal delegates from other nations. These delegates vowed to carry the ashes to their home states and nations and scatter them to the wind with appropriate ceremonies. This was done in Australia, New Zealand, South Africa, and Canada; in every nation of South America; in parts of Europe and Asia; and in all states of the union with the exception of Utah.

COMRADE OR FELLOW WORKER?

[1] Thompson and Murfin, *The IWW*, pp. 169-70, note that twenty medium-size plants were represented by the IWW from 1934-1950. Some of these were Accurate Parts, Draper Steel Barrel, Perfection Metal Container, American Stove, and Republic Brass. Dissaffiliation of the plants from the IWW is discussed on pp. 184-90 and pp. 195-97.

ON THE WATERFRONTS

[1] Thompson and Murfin, *The IWW*, p. 142.

CONTINUED REPRESSION AND DECLINE

[1] Ronald L. McMahon, "Rang-U-Tang: the IWW and the 1927 Colorado Coal Strike," in Joseph Conlin, ed., *At the Point of Production*, pp. 191-212, provides detailed analysis and bibliography of the strike.

A BETTER WORLD

[1] John Graham Brooks, *American Syndicalism: The IWW* (New York: Macmillan, 1913) provides an early account of syndicalist tendencies within the IWW. Haywood liked to differentiate the IWW from its European counterparts, and particularly after 1917, he drew parallels with the Bolshevik outlook. Thus the 1905 IWW call, "All power should rest in a collective membership," was seen as equivalent to the Bolshevik slogan, "All power to the soviets."

[2] None of the major histories of the IWW adequately deal with the IWW involvement in Latin America. A taste of the vast material still largely unorganized can be surmised from the unpublished manuscript of Peter De Shazo and Robert J. Halstead, *Los Wobblies del Sur: The Industrial Workers of the World in Chile and Mexico*, University of Wisconsin-Madison, October 1974. They note, for example, that during the 1920s, at one time or another, the Chilean IWW published ten different newspapers in five cities, making it Chile's most prolific labor organization in terms of publishing. Some Chilean materials were published in Chicago and transported through the MTWU to Chile. The Chilean IWW reached a peak membership of approximately ten thousand.

[3] The IWW involvement in Mexico was more extensive than in any other Latin American nation and remains a story largely untold except in fragments. Ties with Mexican revolutionaries date to the founding of the IWW and in 1911, when the Mexican Liberal party (PLM), an anarchist formation, invaded Baja California in an effort to set up a workers' republic. The campaign was coordinated from an IWW hall in Holtville, California. One hundred IWWs, including Joe Hill, were part of the insurrectionary force. Some Mexican IWWs in Los Angeles opposed the PLM action, but Flores Magon, the PLM's primary leader and now a national hero in Mexico, retained access to the IWW press until his death in the 1920s. During a later phase of the Mexican revolutionary process, IWW locals in Arizona endorsed the Zapata movement and some American Wobblies joined Zapata's armies. After 1917, when the IWW came under federal prosecution, many Wobblies took sanctuary in Mexico to avoid arrest. At one point, there was a plan to have IWW locals headquartered in Mexico, which did not have criminal syndicalist laws. These locals would have been able to organize in border states, reversing the usual pattern of groups headquartered in the U.S. organizing in Mexico

and Canada. IWW miners and marine workers consistently raised the call for an international wage scale as the answer to the problem of lower wages in Latin America causing businesses to migrate south and workers to migrate north. The Mexican IWW remained involved in various strikes, particularly around Tampico, through the 1920s. Two fictional treatments of IWWs in Mexico are Joseph Hergesheimer's *Tampico* and B. Traven's *The Cotton-Pickers*, originally published as *Der Wobbly*.

⁴ Useful data available in G. Jewell, *The IWW in Canada* (Chicago: IWW, 1975), and Jack Scott, *Plunderbund and Proletariat* (Vancouver: New Star Book, 1975).

⁵ Patrick Renshaw, *The Wobblies: The Story of Syndicalism in the United States* (Garden City, NY: Doubleday, 1967). Despite the title, this work is distinguished by its informed coverage of the international influence of the IWW.

⁶ The book was revised with a new chapter on 1955-1975 written by Patrick Murfin. The revised edition has been cited throughout these notes. Thompson has augmented his own writing by advising scholars, gathering archival materials, and helping to arrange interviews with veteran and current IWW members.

INDEX

Solidarity Forever

An Oral History of the IWW

Produced in Chicago by
Americom Type & Design.
Graphic design by Larry Smith
and Russ E. Stoll.

Typeset on the Compugraphic
MCS10/8400 system.
Typefaces are Triumvirate for
heads and Garth Graphic
for body copy.
Printed on acid-free paper.